Software Project Management for Everyday Business

Steve Pye

Contents

Introduction

Twenty-five years ago, I would have classified myself as one of the worst procrastinators on this planet. If there was something I needed to do, I looked for any opportunity to avoid it. I went so far as to avoid doing even the fun things in life, because it was easier and more comfortable to just do absolutely nothing.

Instead of writing a book on project management, I probably could have done well by writing an entire book on how to waste your time and accomplish nothing at all. I'm sure it would not have been very long nor contained much useful information but perhaps that approach would have made a great point.

As I got older though, I started a full-time job doing technical support and working somewhat casually on a handful of software development projects for a company with several hundred employees. There was one other developer working there, and I had the pleasure of muddling my way through those projects without any formal project management training or expertise. This wasn't a software company, so there was no formal software project management process, and although we didn't use the term "waterfall" back then, every project was managed in a waterfall manner, if it was even being managed at all. Most of the time, we had a single goal or outcome, and an empty whiteboard to try to figure out everything that was needed to accomplish that goal.

In doing that work though, it didn't take very long before I realized that working in systems development and management was becoming a real passion of mine. Just enough of a passion to get off the couch and switch to an office chair, which wasn't much of a physical upgrade, but it definitely got my creative juices flowing by being in a professional environment and learning a ton about software development and business processes as I did. It's not everyone's favorite topic, but it became mine.

Continuing with that role, I began devoting much of my spare time to freelance work for a variety of other types of businesses in real estate, education, automotive, construction, technical support, food services, software development, finance, insurance, non-profits, and others. My motivation wasn't financial or career oriented, but rather a combination of pure curiosity and the realization that I was learning far more in those environments than I had learned to date in any educational structures.

Igniting a little bit of passion in me, I realized just how much my natural procrastinating habits were holding me back from getting the full enjoyment out of the work I was doing, and so I set out to find resources and books that would help me overcome that nasty habit. As I read dozens of books on time management, self-improvement, project management, and various systems architecture and business process planning material, I discovered that my natural bent of laziness and procrastination was actually a perfect fuel for being motivated to build technology-based systems. I'd learned that the best system is the one that you can maintain with the least amount of effort, and I was, quite frankly, particularly motivated to find ways to do things with the least possible effort. As a result, I began to love working with systems, and it was just the push I needed to help me overcome what was otherwise such a terrible weakness.

The downside to this, of course, is that I remained—and still do to this day—in a constant state of turmoil as I wrestle with the half of me that wants to do as little work as possible and the other half that is willing to put in twenty-hour days to accomplish great things. Knowing that, however, I discovered that finding the path of least resistance, the quickest route to solve a problem, or the most efficient way to implement a solution became second nature to me, although it was a tremendous amount of work to develop that skill and keep it separate from its evil twin, procrastination. Because of the varied types of businesses I had worked with, my exposure to a wide range of operating methods, organizational structures, and management styles led me to develop a knack for solving problems with well-planned systems, even in fields I had never formally studied.

There are always plenty more areas of opportunity where I can continue learning and growing, and I'm by no means an expert, but the ongoing expertise I've continued to develop has led me to work on small, less impactful projects with the same amount of dedication and determination that I've had working on multi-million dollar projects. Doing this for over two decades now, I've realized that I have reached a point where I can reliably and consistently predict the paths that most projects take from start to finish, and have devised a series of methods for working through a project with due diligence while providing easy ways to step out, pause, or otherwise cancel a project when necessary, with as few negative side effects as possible.

And so, this leads me here, as I begin on what I hope to be a multi-book trek through the finer details of software project management, particularly for those of you who are like me, and are working as a software developer in a company that isn't focused on software development, and you need the administrative and project management skills to properly lead and guide your organization through the ongoing digital revolution of the modern age of business. Instead of facing this journey alone, and having to muddle your way through complex software solutions without any formal project management training, I hope that this book can provide some guidance and direction for you so that you can work through your projects with your health and wellbeing intact.

If you have never done this before, or if you are simply looking to broaden your skills in project management, I hope that you will develop an appreciation for the benefits of following solid, but uncomplicated project management techniques, and applying the more challenging parts of software development to your everyday projects without any damaging side effects. Regardless of your motivation or skill level, and regardless of whether you are administratively minded or not, the principles I'll be going through in this book can apply to almost any software project you need to do, and will give you the guidance and skills you need to plan your project well, communicate on your project's progress, and to complete your projects on time, within budget, and in scope.

There are plenty of opportunities in the future for you to adopt stricter and more formalized project management processes, but for the first few years, the last thing you need as a developer is to spend the majority of your time dealing with politics and bureaucracy and administrative overhead, when all you want to do is write great code and build great systems. If you can commit a few hours to this book and commit to applying these principles in your upcoming work projects, your workload, your time commitment, and your sanity will thank you.

Chapter 1: Why Should I Read This Book?

"Let our advance worrying become advance thinking and planning."
- Winston Churchill

One of the hardest areas of work for software developers to branch into is that of software project management. As software developers it can often be our natural tendency to want to build software above all else, but it can be difficult to see projects through to completion, and to follow standard software development practices when doing development in everyday businesses where your company's primary focus is not development. Many companies just don't want the formality. They simply want their systems built. Trying to build a system without a great plan in place is a common cause of stress, frustration, anxiety, and worry in development. As Winston Churchill put it, "Let our advance worrying become advance thinking and planning." If you want to reduce the stress on your projects, you need to spend more time planning them at the beginning.

Like many forms of project management, software project management has its own complexities and nuances that have to be well-balanced with the work that you're doing. If you are in a management position or if you are the only developer in your company, you may find that management has expectations from you that are difficult for you to provide if your perspective is that of a developer only. This is especially true if you report directly to someone who isn't from the tech industry or who has no experience with software project management or the software development lifecycle.

Common expectations from management levels in an organization include questions like: When will this project be done? How long will the project take? How much will this cost? When can we expect to see some of the deliverables?

As a developer, these kinds of questions can be overwhelming, difficult to answer, and in some cases may even produce a lot of anxiety or worry because you know that once you say how much time something is going to take you'll be held to it with no way out.

So how can you, as a developer, get a better handle on the requirements of project management so that you can serve the needs of your organization well, without making the mistake of unfairly limiting yourself or creating unnecessary stress on your project? If this is a question that rings true for you, then this is the right book for you.

Over the remainder of this book, I will be covering various aspects of the software development lifecycle primarily looking at this from a project manager's perspective, but also providing you with the tools and the skills necessary to properly communicate with your own management team to ensure that you can complete your projects on time, on budget, and with all of the requested features. In many cases, that's considered to be the holy grail in development. It's realistic though, once you realize that project management has less to do with meeting all of the requirements and more to do with managing the expectations of the stakeholders of your project until the project is complete. You'll learn how to cut scope items when necessary with few repercussions while ensuring that you can still deliver a quality project on time and on budget. You'll also learn some great ways to get management buy-in whenever you need to deviate from the requirements. This includes being able to extend the timeline, make budget change requests, change scope items, add more resources to the project, or deliver a result that's quite different from what was originally intended.

But I'm a developer not a project manager! How can I do project management and still get my development work done?

For most developers that I've met, this is a paralyzing situation. There seems to be a general fear that diving into project management will not only take away from development time but also require the developer to spend more of his or her energy dealing with politics rather than doing the work they love. Depending on the nature of the company that you work for, this is a very real possibility. If you manage yourself and your time well enough you can contribute to both the software development requirements and to the project management requirements without having to sacrifice your own discipline in the development realm.

I believe that anyone can be a project manager and you don't need any special training. Just don't tell a certified project manager that!

Understanding project management is just a matter of understanding a few basic core concepts and then learning how to manipulate some variables to your advantage so that you can manage the expectations of your project's stakeholders. You only need to grasp a small handful of concepts and how they interact with each other, and then learn how to use those concepts to communicate effectively with your management team and those working on your project.

It doesn't matter whether you are the only developer or whether you're in charge of an entire team, these principles apply to you and everyone else on the project. As long as you follow the guidelines in this book for each of your development projects, you will learn how to manage expectations and deliver well.

Most importantly, you will learn how to estimate your projects' timelines with relative accuracy and then manage and manipulate the project in a healthy way to see it through to completion. While the thought of estimating is usually anxiety-inducing for a developer, it is important to note that an estimate really is just that... an estimate. If estimates were accurate, they wouldn't be called estimates. They would be called actuals. As you dive into the project management process you will use your estimates as a way of seeking approval for the time that you need to spend on your project. You will also use various techniques to get approval on any scope changes, and then use that as a guideline to discipline yourself and any other developers on your team to ensure that you meet your own deadlines.

My company has no project management office! How can I step in to fill this role?

Believe it or not this is not as hard as you might think. The first step in this whole process is to make sure that the project stakeholders know that you are trying to step in and fill this role. In the absence of a project manager, many companies will welcome a person volunteering to fill a role as long as they also see a need for that role to exist. That can be tricky to validate, but having a predefined process can help to assure others of the validity of the role, and your abilities within it. There are many cases where project management doesn't exist in an organization simply because they don't see a need for that level of bureaucracy, making the assumption that it needs heavy bureaucracy to succeed. I started writing this book because of the number of situations where I encountered exactly that scenario in a company that I was at. The fear of not knowing what is involved in project management can prevent companies from putting a formal project management office in place. But it doesn't need to be that complicated, and this is your opportunity to introduce project management in a simple, straightforward, and healthy way.

Stepping into this role it is important for you to remain humble, which opens the door for others to be more forgiving if you make mistakes. Once you're a professional at this, you won't need to seek as much forgiveness. Beginning with a humility mindset, and identifying that you are there to help solve the gap that your company is currently experiencing is the best way to earn the trust of the people on your team and the people in your organization that you are reporting to.

If this sounds overwhelming to you and you are nervous or anxious about the potential for failure, just remember that you don't have to prove a success… you just have to be able to fail gracefully, learn from your mistakes, and be willing to try again until you get it right. Just having that mindset may be all that's necessary to help get other people in your company on board with adopting project management practices, especially in the software development lifecycle.

My company has unrealistic expectations! How can I educate them about the realities of the development process so that I'm not unreasonably pressured?

This kind of question most frequently comes up when your company is looking for estimates and you either don't know how to estimate properly, or you are afraid that you'll be held to an unrealistic timeline. The first step in addressing this issue is to educate yourself. You've already begun this process by reading this book. The more that you can master the processes of estimating and managing the expectations for your project stakeholders, the easier this will become as you tackle each project that you're given.

Companies can also have unrealistic expectations about deliverables. Specifically, they may expect you to be able to deliver what seems to be an infinitely large scope within an unrealistic timeframe. You can combat this ignorance by soliciting feedback and asking direct questions about what expectations they have and why. When you are given an unreasonably short timeframe, ask what the reason is for being so aggressive on the timing. When you are asked to deliver an unrealistic scope, you should first ask yourself whether it's legitimately unrealistic, or whether it's just unrealistic relative to the resources that you have at your disposal. A large scope is not unrealistic if you have enough people to get the job done. But if you are your company's only developer or where you manage a relatively small team, and the scope expectations are too large, then this is the time to push back and ask whether subcontracting, outsourcing, or even new hires is an option for being able to get the project done on time.

While many developers can fear the thought of outsourcing, knowing that they will be turning over their own work to a third-party that has many more resources available to them, don't be afraid to consider it as an option as long as you are the one responsible for managing that relationship. After all, if you are the only developer or if you represent the development team in your organization, who could possibly be better to manage the relationship with an external development agency or with subcontractors than the person who knows how to do software development directly?

Once you can prove yourself on a few small projects and you can repeat the process every time you're asked to build something new, you will be trusted more and more with the larger projects and trusted with your own estimates on timelines. It's hard to argue when you have factual data to back up your claims. This means you will gain the ability to ensure that your estimates and your actual production times are well aligned. Even though an estimate never represents the actual work time, you can train yourself to ensure that the two are so close that any differences will be considered negligible.

I'm a developer and I'm already the project manager. How do I get everyone else on board with a good project management process?

Your first goal is to establish yourself as the authority in your field. You may already be the authority in development. You may understand the basics for all of the details of the software development lifecycle, regardless of what development process you use, but now you need to establish yourself as an authority in software project management. If you're having trouble getting the rest of your team on board with project management principles, there's a good chance that you're just not being regarded as the authority on this topic.

It never hurts to take the principles outlined in this book and just pass them on to others. You can either teach the principles to other people on your project team and the management team in your organization, or, if they happen to be technically minded it may be wise to even pass on a copy of this book. Although I have written this entire book focused on developers as the readers, I don't dive too heavily into technical concepts such that they would overwhelm a non-technical reader.

So, let's take a look at some of the core principles of project management before we get into the real meat of the project management cycle.

Chapter 2: How can I learn project management concepts quickly?

"Time is the most valuable thing a man can spend."
- Theophrastus

Deep down, most of us want a quick fix when it comes to managing a software project. Taking the time to learn complex principles and concepts when you'd rather be developing is probably the last thing you're motivated to do. And yet, proper planning is essential to having a project succeed, so the more time you devote up front to learning core principles, the better chance you have of succeeding. Of all of the project management variables that you need to account for, time is the single most valuable. Don't try to rush it, just spend it wisely.

Other than time, however, there are two other core constraints that are almost as valuable. Central to most project management systems is a concept referred to as the triple constraint theory. This theory posits that there are three fundamental variables in all project management functions that can be manipulated and adjusted to change the outcome of your project. There is a unique relationship between these three variables in that at least two of them must be adjusted at any given time whenever there is a change. That is, that if one of the variables needs to change then another one must change to compensate. Consider them all to be in a three-way balance. If you adjust one, the project is off-balance, and you need to adjust at least one other variable to balance it back out.

The Triple Constraint Theory -
The Connected Variables

The three variables, as you may have heard before, are time, cost, and quality. Quality is a word that is used sometimes interchangeably with *quantity*—meaning, quantity of features—or also with the term *scope*. In software development, the terms quality, quantity of features, and scope, all effectively refer to the same thing: the actual software deliverables that will be produced in your project.

The basic premise of this model is that the three factors work together in such a way that only two generally apply. Projects that are completed quickly will either be done cheaply, or done well, but not both. Projects that are good and thorough will be either cheap or done quickly, but not both. And similarly, projects that are done cheaply will be either good, or completed quickly, but not both.

As Theophrastus, an ancient Greek philosopher and scientist who studied under Plato declares it, time is commonly considered the most valuable. As a developer you are regularly building much of your system from scratch and the time that it requires for you to write the code is the majority of what's necessary for the project. It's also the one variable that you have to be able to adjust the most since your leadership teams and project stakeholders are most concerned with knowing when your project will be complete. Because of the amount of labor associated with software development, time and cost become interchangeable as well. However, there are other cost factors to take into consideration including costs associated with new hires, outsourcing, subcontracting, and purchasing any frameworks, libraries, or other off-the-shelf products that are necessary to accomplish the project's outcome.

As a general rule, quality is something that you never want to sacrifice in a software project. You do however want to be able to freely make adjustments to the quantity of features or to the scope of the project in order to achieve the desired outcome. Although quality is the term most commonly used in general project management circles, I'll use the term "scope" from this point forward.

The triple constraint theory works with these variables in the following manner. When you need to make an adjustment to one of the variables you automatically must compensate by adjusting another. You can't escape this, so you need to be prepared to respond to adjustments by speaking to one of the other two areas that are affected. Let's look at an example.

Assume for the moment that you are going to complete a project for your company to develop a small product-focused website which is going to be independent from your primary company website. You estimate that you can complete this project by yourself in approximately one month. Let's also assume that as a developer you are paid $60,000 a year and let's ignore other factors such as employer contributions to taxes or other benefits packages so that we can look at your average salary as being just $60,000 dollars to the company. This means one month's worth of work is a cost of $5,000 to the company. Let's also assume that to build this website you're going to offer four primary deliverables as the scope for the project. The nature of those deliverables is irrelevant; what really matters is that you are going to complete four major accomplishments in that one-month timeframe.

Based on this information we can identify that your three variables are as follows:

- Time = 30 days
- Cost = $5,000
- Scope = 4 deliverables/features, (A, B, C, and D)

In establishing these initial variables and estimates, you now submit this to your project owners for approval. As is often the case, they respond back indicating that the cost is too high and that they would like it done in two weeks. From their perspective they believed that by cutting it from 30 days down to 15 the cost should also drop from 5,000 down to 2,500. In theory that could work but the problem is that the cost is based entirely on your labor—one month's worth of your work. In order to complete this project in 15 days you would somehow need to work twice as productively as you currently do. Either that or you need to work overtime effectively putting in 80 hours a week and not receiving any overtime pay.

But here's the key to the triple constraint theory: cutting time in half does not inherently cut the cost in half. In most cases, cutting time requires you to increase cost, not decrease it. With software development, time and scope usually have the more direct relationship. The more time you spend, the more scope you can deliver. The less time you spend, the less scope you can deliver. But when a project is almost fully labor, time and cost act like one variable. It's kind of like a pointer in your favorite programming language. Adjusting one automatically changes the value referenced by the other. In this case, cutting time as a way of cutting cost means that the third variable needs to be adjusted to balance the project, so you also need to cut scope. If they want it done in half the time, they need to cut out half of the deliverables.

The problem with simply cutting time without cutting scope is that you are generally forced to overwork yourself which results in an economic concept that we refer to as diminishing returns. The more hours you put in each day the less productive each of those individual hours becomes. By the time the project is completed you have effectively worked more hours than the original 30 days estimated, because you've had to put in overtime, and you are worn out and exhausted from the project overall, making you less effective on the next project that you're gearing up for. Thus, in order to meet the timeline goal that was imposed on you, you had to donate your time and would have still struggled to complete the entire project in 15 days.

In order to correct this type of pattern you instead need to speak to how the triple constraint theory works, and make sure your supervisors and project owners recognize this. There is an old saying that says that for any job you do, you have three options for how it gets done: having the job done good, fast, or cheap. But you can pick only two. Anything good and fast won't be cheap. Anything good and cheap won't be fast. And anything fast and cheap won't be good. These are the basics of the triple constraint theory.

Knowing this relationship and regularly working to keep the three concepts in balance is necessary for handling a project well. You don't have to know precise numbers, and you don't need to calculate down to the minute, or to the penny, or to the precise number of tasks. You only need to know the relationships between them.

When you were expected to deliver a project in half the time and for half the cost you would have necessarily needed to also reduce the scope. In this particular example time and cost were closely linked because they were associated with your labor. By cutting the time in half you also inherently cut the cost in half, but it necessitated that the scope needed to change to compensate. If the scope had also been cut in half, then the timeline and the cost would have been completely reasonable.

Let's assume for the moment that the cost estimate of $5,000 was acceptable to the project owner, and that only the timing of 30 days was not acceptable. In this case there is an expectation to change one of the variables while having no impact on the other two. Simply deciding that the timeline is not acceptable and that it should be cut in half means that either the cost must double, or the scope must be reduced. This is the nature of the triple constraint theory, in that the following changes must apply:

- To reduce the time, you must increase cost, or decrease scope.
- To increase the scope, you must increase the cost or increase the time.
- To decrease the cost, you must increase the time, or decrease the scope.

The general rule is that in order to achieve a more desirable outcome in one area, you must sacrifice some of the desirable outcome in at least one other area.

This single concept applies to every other factor, variable, and element in project management. If you learn nothing else about project management concepts, this is the most important. Carry this thinking throughout the remainder of this book.

Project Constants - Factors You Have Little to No Control Over

Now that we've covered the variables that are adjustable within a project, let's look at some of the constants that you also face when seeing a project through to completion.

In the example we started with we estimated that the project would take approximately one month with a cost of $5,000 with four core features being delivered. For projects that are only a few days or a few weeks long, those kinds of estimates are reasonably accurate. Once the project requires more than about a month's worth of work or requires effort from multiple people on a team rather than just a single developer, there are other constants that need to be taken into consideration to make the estimate more reasonable.

So, let's use the simple example and add some known constants to strengthen the estimate. In almost any software development scenario, there may be additional resources available to you that will introduce volatility to the estimates you've provided. In this example we were using the case of a small website. If you have enough people on your team, there is a good chance that you have someone dedicated to the graphic design component of the site, a developer dedicated to the coding, and possibly another person dedicated to testing and/or deployment. As soon as you need to start accounting for interconnected resources, such as other people or other teams, you need to add some known constants to your estimates. The four basic constants that you should take into consideration are: slack time, general inaccuracy, business-as-usual, and salaries.

Slack Time

Every employee, no matter how productive will have a certain percentage of slack time that applies to their productivity. You will get to know what that slack time is the more you work with that person. I usually assume that it begins at 10%. Effectively this means that a person spends up to four hours a week not directly focused on productive work. This may be mandatory break time, water cooler chats, bathroom breaks, getting coffee, or simply moving back and forth between meetings. You might be surprised at how quickly it adds up when you measure it.

Then you need to add any mandatory vacation time for your particular region or employment structure. Assuming that your company or region's vacation policy is two weeks per year, this represents 4% of a person's overall time. (2 weeks ÷ 52 weeks = 4%).

Then, add any statutory holidays applicable to your area. Let's assume there are 10 statutory holidays in a year. Ten days is another two weeks, so this represents another 4%.

You should also account for any average sick time that is generally applicable to your office. Some experience it more than others, due to the number of employees who have school-aged children, the general health of people in your area, whether your company provides health-related benefits, and so forth. You may be able to get this information from your HR department. This can simply be expressed as a percentage of the person's work hours, just like we do with vacation time. Let's assume that the average person is sick for a total of two weeks each year, for another 4% added to the slack time.

Overall, this results in your total slack time being 22% (10% + 4% + 4% + 4%).

General Inaccuracy

Somewhat similar to slack time you will also have a general inaccuracy factor that you should add to any estimates. Although slack time covers common productivity interruptions like coffee breaks, it generally applies to everyone in the company equally. The inaccuracy factor might be unique to each person or to each team. This factor is somewhat loosely based on an old idea that whatever your estimates are you should double them before you reveal them to anyone. Yet, arbitrarily doubling your estimate is not a mature way to calculate realistic values, so this shouldn't be your go-to method. Once someone realizes that every estimate you gave is automatically being doubled, they will assume that your estimate needs to be cut in half every time. Instead, if you can provide specific values to explain a padded estimate, your estimates will be taken more seriously. I will usually assume an inaccuracy rate of 25%. This is derived from two factors:

First, I account for a typical person's production capacity outside of slack time. The 10% base value in slack time is non-productive time. But capacity is a person's ability to produce within their productive time, which is unique to them. One developer might be a high producer who focuses well, while another is just plain slow. But both need to get water, use the washroom, or walk to a meeting, and those shouldn't be considered part of their productivity. Based on that, I've found that most people, irrespective of slack time, simply do not produce at 100% capacity for every hour they are sitting at their desk. There will always be moments where slack time doesn't apply, and they are sitting at their desk working, but not necessarily being productive. Or at the very least, they are not being productive on the project that they're allocated to.

Second, people are generally bad at estimating. When estimating time, many people will simply not take enough variables or external factors into consideration and will probably underestimate their time. Having a little bit of flexibility by padding their estimate for them will help with this. As they continue to get more accurate in their estimating, you can always adjust this percentage for their work.

Business as Usual

Slack time accounts for non-working time that an employee is still paid for. The inaccuracy factor accounts for actual working time that was miscalculated relative to productivity. The business-as-usual (BAU) constant accounts for work time that is productive but that is spent on projects other than the project you are primarily focusing on. For software developers, this can include addressing bugs or issues with existing software, troubleshooting, or meetings about other projects. Unlike slack time and the inaccuracy factor, which affect your effort estimates automatically, the BAU factor will help to pad your estimate to align with your project's duration estimate. I'll cover the difference between effort and duration in chapter four. In the meantime, just remember that the BAU percentage will differ from person to person and company to company, but once you have a number you can always adjust it over time as the conditions change. Starting with 20% or 25% is decent, as that generally represents about eight to ten hours in any given week.

Salaries

Lastly, you will want to account for salaries as constants as well. If you're managing a team, you probably know the salaries of both yourself and your team members. You may or may not know other teams, but for whatever you do know, it's good to make a note of it. This is so that when you estimate hours on a project, you have a rough idea of what the cost per hour is, which can give you an estimate on the project's overall cost. This can be helpful when negotiating with subcontractors or other third parties, or when comparing the cost of developing a solution against the cost of purchasing an off-the-shelf product.

If possible, you should also consider the actual salary cost to the organization, not just your specific gross salary. Depending on where you live, your employer may also contribute to local or federal taxes, employment insurance, health benefits, retirement plans, or other monetary costs that may be a percentage of your wage, or some easily calculable value that you can account for. Since that represents a cost that is more accurate for the cost to the company, if you are able to access that information, you should pad each person's salary with that percentage so that you have a more accurate hourly wage. I generally like to make a reasonable assumption that the real cost to a salary is between 25% and 50% higher than the real dollars of the salary.

* * *

For each of the constants above, you should keep these numbers readily available. Going back to our month-long project example, this is how you would apply these factors to your estimate:

The initial estimate was:

- Time = 30 days
- Cost = $5,000
- Scope = 4 features

Constants:

- Slack time = 22% (10% water cooler, 4% vacation, 4% statutory holidays, 4% sick time)
- Inaccuracy factor = 25%
- Business-as-Usual = 25% (assuming you spend about 10 hours a week doing other normal daily tasks)
- Salary = 130% (assuming your employer must pay 30% of your salary towards benefits and taxes).

Your new time estimate will be (note that these values are compounded):

```
= ((30 days + 22%) + 25%) + 25%
= (36.6 days + 25%) + 25%
= 45.75 days + 25%
= 57.2 days
```

Your new cost estimate will be:

```
= ($5,000 / 30) x 57.2  --> This is because your time
changed.
= $166.67 x 57.2
= $9,533
```

The reason that we compound the time values, is because slack time is a mandatory number, so inaccuracy and BAU are impacted by it. We compound BAU on to inaccuracy, because we tend to neglect to allocate enough time to doing business as usual like we should. In other words, BAU efforts are often inaccurate and need be expanded marginally.

In the end, your original estimate of 30 days and $5,000 should have been almost 60 days, and about $9,500. Not only does this give you a more realistic number that accounts for holidays and sick time, among other factors, it also paints a better picture for you on whether your project requires alternative options to be considered. It's important to note at this point that we are starting to determine a comparison between your effort estimate (30 days) and the practical or duration estimate (60 days) which more accurately represents the timeline. This discrepancy is vital to understanding estimating! I'll cover the specifics of this part of estimating in chapter four.

So How Do I Move Forward with this Knowledge?

Now that you have the basics of the project management concepts and estimating covered, you need to implement three habits to help make your project a success.

Habit 1: Get Good, Fast

"We become what we repeatedly do."
- Stephen Covey

It is important to be able to apply project management principles quickly and consistently through your project. Seeing a project through to completion is the best way to get a good handle on how to treat all future projects. Make the disciplines in this book a priority and apply them to every project you do, no matter how small. Taking the time to practice this regularly is the best way to get good at it quickly.

Habit 2: Track Everything

"If you can't measure it, you can't improve it."
- Peter Drucker

You should always keep three tools readily accessible to you. First a good text editor on your computer. Although it can be tempting to use an advanced program such as a mind mapping tool, a word processor, or even some basic project management software, nothing beats the speed and performance of a solid text editor. You won't get hung up on dealing with things like formatting or text alignment or having to fill in values in a project management program that are unnecessary for your project. Try to select a text editor that provides cloud syncing options so that you have access to your notes on multiple devices, and so that your notes are automatically saved as you go. Document everything you can think of and keep it all in a single file or multiple files in a single folder for each project.

Second, you should have a spreadsheet easily accessible where you can track key pieces of data where searching, sorting, and reorganizing the data may be necessary. You even have access to some quick functions to do fancy calculations for you. For instance, you may want to keep track of project meeting dates and times, and you will want to keep those values in different spreadsheet columns so that you can sort and search easily. Use your text editor to keep track of all of your notes but put the most important highlights into a spreadsheet so that you can quickly scan through the critical items and times when needed.

Lastly, get a good handheld notebook. Actual paper, not a digital one. As an IT professional you're probably tempted to use a digital notebook. Try to resist this temptation until you have enough project experience behind you that you can use the digital tools effectively. Our brains are well wired to remember what we hand write more easily than what we type, so to get into good habits, you should start with pen and paper. Furthermore, a notebook and pen can always go with you wherever you go, but a computer, tablet, or mobile device may not always be as accessible as they appear to be. Spotty Wi-Fi, sync problems, or even meetings where you're asked to keep your phone off happen just frequently enough that you'll wish you used a physical notebook at least a couple of times during your project. You can always transfer your notes into your text editor at a later time if you wish, or use OCR software if you have it available.

Habit 3: Communicate Proactively, Not Reactively

This is probably the most important habit. Always have a communication plan for every project to make sure that you keep stakeholders, shareholders and owners apprised of any details that they need to know as they happen. If you don't get in the habit of communicating proactively, you'll be stuck communicating reactively to every issue that crops up, and in those cases you may find yourself giving answers you will regret. It's always better to be prepared in advance with the answers that are needed before you are caught off guard by someone who then makes your day miserable. You're thinking of someone right now, aren't you?

What Are My Goals?

Now that you have at least a rough idea of what variables and constants to take into consideration when estimating a project, you need to ensure that you have some specific project goals to work towards as your project progresses. Inevitably one or more of these variables will change through the course of your project, and unless you know what your project management goals are—and note that these are not the goals of the project itself—you will be better equipped to adjust the variables to compensate for the changes.

Your project goals apply to all projects, and these are goals that you would impose on yourself as both a developer and as a project manager. These are the administrative goals of all projects.

Goal number one: deliver your project on time, on budget, and on scope.

Goal number two: get permission and approval for all changes.

Goal number three: maintain excellent logs so that you can revise the values used in your constants to increase accuracy on future projects and reduce assumptions.

Goal number four: manage the expectations on the project, not the people.

Goal number five: always have a mindset of learning.

Keep these goals top-of-mind for all of your projects and remember to hold yourself accountable to these results.

How Do I Make My Projects Successful? Or, How Do I Win?

If you want to win at your project you need to finish well. Sometimes that means getting all the way to the end and completing all of the goals above. Other times it may mean accepting defeat and recognizing that you won't achieve one or more of the goals. So, when you do fail, you need to fail gracefully. Consider it like graceful degradation or exception-handling for your administration efforts.

Be humble. Be willing to take the blame when things go wrong, but take the necessary steps to overcome the failure and to prevent it from happening again. Communicate that plan to others.

Don't forget to celebrate others' victories. When managing a project, you need to be willing to take the blame when it fails but to give the credit to others when it succeeds.

Ask lots of questions. It may be easier to get forgiveness than permission, but getting permission puts the decision-making responsibility on others, and allows you to continue working through your plan without deviation while you leave the tougher choices up to others to answer.

Since you are logging everything as it happens, make sure you always follow-up with any affected people for every decision that's made. Solicit constant feedback and be willing to make adjustments as you go.

If you're ready to work like this, then you're ready to start managing your first project like a boss.

Chapter 3: The Five Phases of a Software Project

"An intelligent plan is the first step to success. The man who plans knows where he is going, knows what progress he is making and has a pretty good idea when he will arrive. Planning is the open road to your destination. If you don't know where you are going, how can you expect to get there?"
- Basil S. Walsh

Now that we've covered the basics of some general project management terms, it can be helpful to see a map of how the project management lifecycle fits into the software development lifecycle. Regardless of what software development methodology you normally use, there are five basic phases of the development process that are fairly consistent:

1. Planning
2. Analysis
3. Design
4. Implementation
5. Maintenance

Similarly, most projects follow a similar lifecycle:

1. Initiating
2. Planning
3. Execution
4. Control
5. Closure

These are from a popular method referred to as the IPECC method. Other methodologies, such as JPACE, use a similar structure.

While the project management phases are not necessarily a direct match to common software development phases, there is still an underlying approach where the project is produced first as an idea, then as a plan, then the plan is implemented, managed, and closed when complete. Unless you have an expectation to follow that basic plan from beginning to end, you can safely assume that you will encounter challenges and frustration along the way. Following the plan won't always guarantee that you won't be frustrated, but it will reduce the stress and help to give you the skills to ensure you can make it to the end with your wits intact. As Basil Walsh puts it, "if you don't know where you are going, how can you expect to get there?" The plan, whether perfect or not, is still your best guide to getting your project done.

In the years that I have spent doing both software development and general project management in companies that focus on software development as well organizations that do not have development as their core discipline, I've regularly needed to merge the concepts of structured software development processes with the basics of project management requirements in order to have other project managers get on board with the software process with minimal retraining.

Chances are if you are working for an organization that doesn't have software development at its core, you will need to be able to work through the software development process while communicating in business terms to the project stakeholders. This usually means sacrificing some of the more bureaucratic processes of the software development lifecycle in favor of following a more business focused cycle. Just like the example five phases of project management and five phases of software development that I listed above, I tend to follow a five-phase process that helps to merge good development practices with business focused project management techniques. I would stress that these five phases are not necessarily ideal for extraordinarily large software development operations or for organizations that already have a software development lifecycle in place. Specifically, you probably don't want to use this to manage the build of a new operating system, or a massive commercial application like Microsoft Office, or Salesforce. But they are ideal for an organization where software development is not the primary focus, or for software companies that are building initially smaller-scale applications, and especially where there are one or more people in your IT department who are focused on developing and delivering custom developed business solutions for your organization or its customers.

The five phases of this process are as follows:

1. Assessment and Estimating
2. Planning and Architecture
3. Development
4. Testing and Deployment
5. Maintenance and Growth

ASSESSMENT & ESTIMATING	PLANNING & ARCHITECTURE	DEVELOPMENT	TESTING & DEPLOYMENT	MAINTENANCE & GROWTH
Scope and Estimates / Qualifications	Brainstorming / Analysis / Design	Organizing Architecture / Building / Coding / Reviewing / Testing	Staging / User Acceptance / Training / Deployment	Support / Maintenance / Growth

Each of these phases has multiple sections within it, and multiple tasks within each section. Note that these are project management tasks, not development tasks. While many of the tasks represent aspects of development, this is meant to provide a mid-level view of what's needed for a project, and it's up to individual developers to break down the project requirements and identify a to-do list of deliverables that properly represents the code and the programming work that's required. This provides a great framework for knowing whether you have all of the proper requirements in place so that the development effort can be determined properly and carried out as needed.

Phase 1 Overview: Assessment and Estimating

The first of these five phases can be the most overwhelming and most paralyzing phase for developers, especially if they are primarily responsible for product delivery. In all my years of development with companies, the number one question that I am asked at any phase in a project is, "when will the software be done?" Or some variation of that question. So, the idea of doing upfront assessment and estimating is something that a lot of developers tend to shy away from, since it has a tendency to backfire on them.

In one company where I worked, one of the owners had a habit of wandering over into the development area, targeting a specific developer, and asking, "where are we at?" While many of the developers would frantically try to explain what they were working on at that precise moment, we always knew the owner's next question would inevitably be, "can we have something to show the customer by Friday?" Or some such day. It also wasn't uncommon for this to be asked on Thursday afternoon. While this wasn't generally a problem for most people on the team, many of the projects we were all concentrating on had such a loose definition up front that developers regularly produced some kind of a Western-front implementation that satisfied the customer's customized request, which bought us enough additional time to build out the software correctly.

All too often though, after building that demo presentation, the customer would back out of the deal for an unrelated reason, so it seemed that the developers were just building that Western-front because they knew they'd eventually be throwing the code away. Why bother estimating or planning anything properly if you know you're just wasting your time? But I noted, as the project manager working there, that once the owner was satisfied with the timeline—realistic or otherwise—and walked away, almost every developer would then breathe a sigh of relief, knowing they'd just been cornered on a deliverable, and managed to get out of it.

Overall though, this response from developers did more harm than good. While it did deflect the situation, and pacify an executive, it did nothing for keeping morale high, and ultimately sent a message to the executive that this behavior was being affirmed. Yet, developers were still frequently feeling on edge and stressed, and felt as though they were being monitored for their performance in an overtly aggressive way. As I continued to refine the processes that I used to help make development smoother, I also started looking deeper into different methods of communicating project progress to help prevent some of those uncomfortable questions of "where are we at" from management.

The more I reviewed and tested different communication methods, the more I found variations between how software companies differ from everyday businesses. Specifically, in a software company, there's usually a much better understanding of the standard development processes at a high level. In a non-software company, everything that is "geek speak" has to be translated into business terminology to be understood. This sank in for me when I realized, at that software company, that the person asking the questions was the one executive who didn't fully understand the development process. Another executive who did, was the one who never asked those kinds of questions, and usually spoke in defense of the process to the other executive. This is why it's so important, as a project manager, to speak in defense of your processes, communicate well, and help your executives and other managers to fully understand you and your team's needs.

Regardless of the environment, there was always one question that regularly came up, and was the cause of the most anxiety in developers: some variation of, "when will it be done?" The assessment and estimating phase of a project can cause that point of anxiety for a developer, because it suggests that they will be held to some premature commitment that they can't reasonably accomplish. Knowing how to assess and estimate properly, and how to communicate that to your company's leaders, will make all the difference on how comfortable you and your team will feel working through the rest of the project. I'll cover the full details of assessment and estimating in chapter four.

But estimates are bunk! How can I assess and estimate correctly?

It's a common belief that development estimates are basically garbage, and should be ignored, but there are two advantages to doing estimates in development anyway. First, they give you the opportunity to establish a timeline that provides more than enough breathing room to account for variances, while still being close enough to reality that you don't come across as a terrible estimator. When it's done well, you can communicate valid logic behind an estimate that's mostly irrefutable, because it's based on a calculation, rather than on a wild guess. Second, they are a great way to give project stakeholders and managers some visibility into the work you do, which improves communication. That improvement in communication translates to a better workflow between you and project owners, which can help the project run more smoothly, even if it's going off the rails.

I like to stick with the idea that estimates are only correct for as long as they're only mostly correct. Let me explain.

By the nature of an estimate, you can't estimate correctly. If you could, then you'd be able to see the future, and you probably wouldn't be working where you are. An accurate estimate happens either by complete fluke, or, because the estimate wasn't an estimate, it was an actual. The latter is borderline prophetic, and we don't assume that to be true.

When you estimate a software project, what you are doing is establishing your parameters and then setting a framework for you to work within to help focus your process. Your job isn't to establish the perfect estimate. Your job is just to establish an estimate that can get approved by the project owner, and to maintain a pattern for adapting to changes as they are needed.

Phase 2 Overview: Planning and Architecture

Phases two through to four will be the more measurable parts of your project. As a guideline, each phase should consume about one-third of the project's time, and each section within those phases will consume about one-third of that time. Regardless of what workflow methodology you use for your development, using this as a guideline helps to give you a safe baseline for how long you're spending on your development process, and whether you're staying on track. Starting with the Planning and Architecture phase, you can expect that this will take about one-third of the time. If your project is three months long, expect to spend a month in this phase. Use it as a guideline, not a fixed rule.

I've met three kinds of developers in my career, relative to development and architecture. There are those who have a natural ability to architect software solutions well. Most of those developers work towards an architectural role, and then stick with architecture for the remainder of their software career. Then there are those who fully understand architectures, and can build software solutions according to architecture plans, and do a good job at it, but couldn't design an architecture from scratch. Lastly, there are developers who simply have no expertise with creating or understanding complex architectural patterns but are still experts at implementing great development solutions. There aren't any good developers who have zero understanding of architecture, because even the ability to write a function that takes one piece of data and converts it to another format is a basic representation of an architecture pattern known as an adapter.

The latter two types of developers are the ones who commonly struggle the most with this phase, because architecture patterns don't come naturally to them. If you're in this category, chapter five will be particularly helpful for you, but for now, let's look at the high-level issue with developers and architecture. That is, that the two disciplines, while closely related, are not the same skillset.

I'm a developer, not an architect! How am I supposed to plan and architect an entire project?

Your first focus should be on learning architectural patterns. Chances are, if you've had any amount of higher education in software development, you've been introduced to a standard set of architectural patterns at some point in your training. If you haven't, or if you need to brush up them, I recommend reading *Design Patterns: Elements of Reusable Object-Oriented Software* by Erich Gamma, Richard Helm, Ralph Johnson, and John Vlissides. While this book was written some time ago, in 1995, the architecture patterns remain foundational to pretty much every software project you could envision. The concepts are timeless, and the authors, affectionately referred to as "The Gang of Four" have provided material that will serve you well in architecting software solutions. If nothing else, using that book as a reference for terminology in architecture design can help to bring credibility to any solutions you propose, because you can quote the pattern as a guideline for whatever solution you are working on. Learn the patterns outlined in that book, and how to reuse them.

When turning basic architectural patterns into a solid architecture for your project, you will normally use a combination of one or more individual patterns to create a pattern that is unique to the business issue that you need to solve for your organization.

When planning, keep the plan simple, and worry about the more detailed aspects of it when you get there. Consider this planning phase to be a 30,000-foot view. If you've flown in an airplane, you have undoubtedly seen farmland from the sky, with varying amounts of green, brown, yellow, and other colors scattered for miles. From that high up, it's relatively easy to look at a large area of land and decide that you want to move an entire field and swap it with another field. Take this brown field from here, and move it to this green field over here, and take that green field and move it where the brown field is.

Realistically, this is an absurd example, but from a high-level view like that, it appears conceptually simple. Just plow away chunks of the field and swap them. To an implementer, knowing that they have to keep each blade of grass, or each rock, in the same relative position when swapping the two fields makes this a far more complicated project than how it looks from high up. It's not uncommon for management to only see the 30,000-foot view and at that height everything seems simple, so it's now your job to make sure that they understand that just because it looks simple from a high-level view, doesn't mean it's simple in implementation.

It's okay to cater to those beliefs though, but always remember what kind of real work it takes to accomplish it. It won't happen in a couple of days.

To help establish that high-level plan and communicate it well, you need to turn to the specific experts who will be carrying out the actual work. Yielding to their expertise helps you to put a plan in place that is realistic, even though it may be overwhelming to start. If you're the only expert, but you're not an architecture expert, getting good at architecture is a goal you should set for yourself.

Phase 3 Overview: Development

Development is the phase where you're probably going to shine the most, because that's already your strength. But when you're doing development and managing the project, you're going to be constantly snapping back and forth between the high-level view and the low-level tasks that are necessary to accomplish the implementation. This kind of back-and-forth work can be mentally draining, and difficult to regularly translate technical details into high-level concepts so that your company's leadership can understand it well. In much the same way that language translators (real world languages, like English and Mandarin, not software languages) can experience a lot of mental stress when doing translations for long period of time, as a developer you're likely to experience some kind of burn out when you need to constantly translate your technical issues into business issues while also trying to deal with all of the finer points of implementation.

That means you'll need to spend a fair bit of time regularly reviewing your technical operations, and comparing them to your estimates and your architecture, so that you can provide suitable status updates that are related to the business needs, and not just to your technical requirements.

When you do get off course, you're likely going to need to translate the issues into a suitable business explanation, so it's better to be prepared for that ahead of time.

Alright, I'm willing to learn how to do that high-level plan, but how do I ensure that plan stays on course during the development process?

The most important thing you can focus on during the development phase is communication. Make a point to meet with your team of developers regularly. If you're a lone wolf developer, meet with your business associates and other project stakeholders regularly. Keep them informed of the process as you go, and make sure they have a good understanding of where you're at, and how it's going.

When doing development, it can help to use an iterative approach to the process, where you develop multiple iterations of functions and classes, with increasing levels of perfection each time. For instance, on your first build of a complex function, just have the function produce precisely the output you expect it to produce. Use that to run tests to verify that the function is working properly in context, then iterate through the function to create explicit exceptions and errors based on known conditions. Eventually, the final product will include full exception handling that will accept the proper input, provide the expected output, and exception gracefully when there's a problem. This approach gives a fast, up-front test, and also gives you the opportunity to present working prototypes of your work early on in the process so that your project stakeholders can see progression. This is particularly valuable when doing API development, or when building web services for your system to use.

Steve Jobs regularly used a similar technique in the various Apple Keynotes where he presented new products, such as the introduction of the first iPhone. Rather than attempting to show a single phone that did everything they claimed, he had multiple phones connected to the presentation screen, with each one ready to perform the exact demonstration he needed. Instead of fumbling through broken areas of the premature system he was presenting, he prepared each phone to perform only the single task he was looking to present at that moment. When one failed, he simply grabbed the next working phone and moved on. Taking this approach in development and applying to iterative releases gives you the opportunity to present a fully working system to your development team and your users, soliciting feedback along the way, while also ensuring that the majority of the functional code is in place so that you only need to fill in the details to finish it off.

Phase 4 Overview: Testing and Deployment

This is another area you're already going to be fairly good at, unless you're like basically every other developer I've met, including the one in my mirror. Testing is one of those necessary evils that we generally do by just tossing the system out into production and waiting for the bug reports. I get it. Testing isn't a lot of fun, and unless you have a great budget available to you, you probably don't have many formal test scripts with Git hooks and continuous integration and nightly builds. If you're the only developer, chances are your idea of a test is to pop in to a UI, try to enter a piece of bad data, and if it fails correctly, you're good to go, right?

We all know that testing is needed, so why do we sacrifice that so much when we're operating at a company where the person in charge of us isn't literally looking over our shoulder waiting for the nightly build report to find out what needs to be fixed?

If you've followed the development process above though, and developed your system iteratively, there's a good chance you've already caught most of the bugs. Without fail though, there are going to be many that slip through the cracks and make it into production no matter how diligent you are.

Alright, let's assume I can develop iteratively and keep my project on track. What happens when I want to go live, and I'm not quite ready?

If you want to be able to test and deploy like a boss, get good at scripting, and using automated deployment solutions. Chances are, if you're an experienced developer, you already have these tools at your disposal, or you have a system such as Microsoft's .NET platform that has deployment processes baked into the development environment.

If you're a small team, or a team of one, or if you have a relatively small set of tools at your disposal, using scripting processes can speed up your testing and deployment process. In many of the smaller companies that I've worked with, software deployment—especially for web applications—was a single developer copying code from their machine to a server using a local FTP application. There's huge potential for human error, and more time spent fixing file copy errors and permissions than would have been spent using a script that handled the deployment automatically. Building scripts means you get to do more programming anyway, just in the testing phase, so what's stopping you from automating?

You may also need to be willing to implement a multi-operating system solution, and virtualization, to take advantages of environments like PowerShell or Bash to perform deployments, especially if you can do it directly from the master branch of your source control system.

If you don't have the luxury of implementing more expensive solutions, don't be afraid to identify large solutions that you require, as part of your company's big projects, so that you can secure some extra budget money to upgrade or enhance a server in the process. If the company is willing to pay you $30,000 to develop a custom solution over a six-month period, they are probably going to be open to you adding a $6,000 server in the process that will help you deliver this project, and several future projects, in less time.

Phase 5 Overview: Maintenance and Growth

Okay, this sounds like something I can tackle. What about maintenance and growth, though? How do I account for that in my project?

No matter how finished you think your project is, you're going to need to maintain it over time. Even if the system itself is complete, the platform it runs on is going to change, and you're going to need to consider some kind of transition strategy to retire your system in favor of a newer replacement.

Up front, you may not always need to identify the cost of maintenance long-term. But it is a good idea to add it to your percentage of BAU work that you handle on a regular basis. If you expect to spend 5% of your annual time maintaining the software you developed, you should add that 5% to the BAU that you normally account for when estimating a project's overall duration. Eventually, you'll reach a point where the demands on your time, or your team's time, will exceed the amount of time your team has available by enough of a percentage that it justifies hiring more members for your team. At a minimum, you should be raising that issue whenever your maintenance time is more than 33% of your overall available time. By 50%, you should be looking at hiring, because now you're spending more time maintaining than you are building, which has the potential to become costly.

In your ongoing growth planning, it also helps to regularly assess the cost of maintaining your system against the cost of replacing it with a common, off-the-shelf product. It may be that your company needs the development done up front, but over the years, an existing product might surface that will fulfill the same need and will free up your maintenance time long-term. Don't be afraid to propose swapping out the systems and freeing up more time for you to focus on new projects.

If you also keep a backlog for any maintenance work and do regular comparisons of your estimates and actuals for the time spent on the project, you'll have a better handle on the ongoing use of your time.

Chapter 4: Phase 1 - Assessment and Estimating

How can I estimate accurately?

Of the five phases of the project lifecycle, I've found that a common difficult phase for developers and IT professionals to master is the assessment and estimating phase. There are many variables to consider, and just enough unknowns to make the estimating process overwhelming. Developers tend to shy away from committing to estimates because they feel unnecessarily handcuffed to a timeline just because someone asked for a delivery date, and now expect it to be met. And yet, the pressure to meet a manufactured deadline still happens regularly, so how do we work through the estimating challenges without feeling bullied or pressured? An agile project is one of the easiest ways to commit to manageable deadlines, since they are generally only two weeks in length, but there is still a common expectation that a project is planned and estimated as a waterfall project before it begins, which can start the project off with a lot of anxiety for developers.

There's an old saying that asks, "How do you eat an elephant?" And the answer to that is, "one bite at a time." Attributed to Creighton Abrams, a US army general, his point was solid: when you are trying to take on a task that is particularly difficult or overwhelming, take it slowly, and break it down into smaller, more manageable parts. Initially, the thought of consuming an entire elephant is overwhelming, just like the thought of seeing a large development project through to the end and putting estimates to everything. But if you employ a "one bite at a time" mentality, the process is not quite as exhausting.

As you'll see in all of the remaining chapters, I try to break down each phase into manageable sections and tasks which can be dealt with one at a time, until the project is done. And to make the process easier for those of you with a software development mindset, I've approached each section within the phase using a philosophy of inputs and outputs, with single-step tasks to achieve the result.

For this phase, there are two sections: Scope and Estimates, and Qualifications. The entire assessment and estimating phase can take anywhere from a few hours, to several days or even weeks, depending on the size of the project. Overall, I'd say that about one-fifth of a project's total time is spent in this phase. You don't normally need to include time spent in this phase in your estimate, since it would be silly to estimate the time required to do estimates, only to add your estimated time to your estimate. Your brain would collapse in on itself before you'd even get started.

So, one bite at a time, let's work through these phases and outline the requirements.

Section 1.1: Scope and Estimates

Inputs:

- The project request, or project idea.

Steps:

- Identify the project's scope
- Estimate a baseline effort
- Quantify the tasks
- Normalize the tasks
- Prioritize the tasks

Outputs:

- Preliminary Scope document
- Effort Estimate

In this section of phase one, the outcome we expect is to turn a project idea into a preliminary scope, with some initial effort estimates. You need the scope to determine the effort, and you need the effort to get ultimate approval on moving ahead with the project. Note that the effort is the total number of person-hours required to accomplish the project, as opposed to the actual dates and times when the project will be completed. If you assume something will take ten days to accomplish, you have to add clarity on that to ensure that people realize that it means ten business days, which is more precisely two weeks. Three, in fact, if you don't plan on deploying your completed solution at 5pm on a Friday. Having the initial estimates upfront helps you to qualify the project before you have to start doing design and development.

Identify the Scope

It is common for a project to be submitted with either an incomplete scope, or, if your project owner is a thorough person, a potentially overcomplicated scope. But rarely does the scope identify the actual software development requirements. Instead, the scope will just define the business need or the outcome that the requester is expecting from you.

It's a good idea to read through their scope request, assuming they wrote it out, and identify as many key deliverables as you can. Specifically, if you were to rewrite their scope request as a feature list for your software, what would you identify?

Once you have the full list of scope items identified in the form of software features, approach any of the implementers who are best suited to give you an estimate on how long each key feature should take. If you're the only person in your IT department who handles development, then all of this will fall on you. As long as you aren't bound by confidentiality policies, it never hurts to solicit some input from other developer associates or friends you know who can provide some third-party validation of your initial estimates.

If you've never done estimating before, I'll cover the easiest starting point for you.

Estimating a Baseline Effort

When doing your first formal estimate, it doesn't hurt to just start with a wild guess! If nothing else, it gives you a starting point to work with, and you can always refine your estimate later. An easy method I've used with my own development teams, which is generally accurate enough to work with, is to ask for what I call a "T-estimate." I have them give a gut-level guess based on one of five different units of time, identified by a value, T.

T1 is one hour. T2 is one day. T3 is one week. T4 is one month. T5 is one year. If you're not sure, start with the absurd. Do you think this feature (scope item) will take a year to accomplish? It's rare for average company projects to take one or more years, but it's not unheard of either. Even if they think it would take two years, your estimate is just a T5, because you're expressing your estimate in "units of T." Although you can always be a little more specific and estimate two years. Anything from one to seven hours is T1. Anything from one to four days is T2. You can get more specific when you know more. When you are talking about individual features rather than the project as a whole, a T5 is a particularly absurd estimate. If the reply to the question, "do you think this will take a year?" is simply, "no," then you ask the next question. Do you think this will take a month? And on you go, down to the hour, until you get some kind of gut-instinct estimate.

Let's assume, though, that your expert, which might just be yourself, says, "it definitely won't take a year, but it will take longer than a month." You can get more specific: six months? No, I think it will be less than six. Three months? No, maybe two. Voila! You now have a reasonable estimate. You can either be specific, and mark it as "two months," or you can stay generic and use "greater than T4 but less than T5," which effectively means, more than a month but less than a year. Still a bit absurd, but the process can yield a fairly decent starting point. If there's a lot of uncertainty, estimating as just "T4" (meaning, it could take one or more months) is perfectly fine.

If your expert is a little more specific though, as many want to be, they might even supply you with a range, such as, "I think this could take anywhere from six to eight weeks to implement." In this case, it's usually good to pick the 75% mark of that range. So, take the difference between the two, two weeks, and find out 75% of that. Two weeks is 10 days. 75% of that is 7.5 days. Round it up just to be safe. So, you're going to assume the low value (six weeks) plus about eight more days. You can even narrow it down to identify six weeks as being more precisely 30 business days (6 x 5 days), which means your estimate will be about 38 days. Don't worry about the precision here. You're looking for a baseline estimate, not an actual value, and you certainly don't need to immediately report to management that your first scope item will take 38 days. That's just your effort estimate, and you still have some padding to account for.

Repeat this estimating process for all of the major scope items that were identified, so that you can put the number of days beside each scope item.

Now, remember all of the additional constants I mentioned back in chapter two? You now want to take the total of all of your estimates and add the percentages from your constants. In the example we used at the beginning, we determined that we needed to add 22% slack time, 25% for an inaccuracy factor, and another 25% to account for BAU. Now it's time for a little bit of math. For the single scope item identified above, where we estimated 38 days, we now calculate the baseline duration estimate:

```
= ((38 + 22%) + 25%) + 25%
= (46.36 + 25%) + 25%
= 57.95 + 25%
= 72.44 days
```

What you want to record here, preferably in a spreadsheet where you can apply the math easily, is that your baseline effort estimate was 38 days, but your reasonable duration estimate is about 72.5 days. This effectively means that although a best-guess is that it should require about 38 days to achieve this specific feature, most people will have given an estimate assuming that nothing else happens and that they can devote 100% of their time to the project. Since that's rarely the case, you're effectively padding their estimate and making it 72.5 days instead.

Duration differs from your effort estimate, in that a duration estimate identifies approximately how long it should take to complete your project, with a fairly accurate degree of reasonableness. This differs from effort, because effort only identifies the amount of productive work time needed to accomplish the project. For instance, if you were to estimate that a project requires 40 hours of work, then in theory, you could start the task at 7am on a Monday, and you would be done by 11pm on Tuesday night, if you assume that you can work 40 hours non-stop. That, of course, is unrealistic. In most circumstances, 40 hours of work would require a full work week from Monday to Friday. Depending on whether the project's tasks can be done by more than one person at a time, you might even be able to get it done by noon on Wednesday if you have two people working on it. Further, you need to assume that you won't be 100% productive for all 40 hours, and that's where the above calculations apply, allowing you to take your reasonable effort estimate (the labor required to accomplish the tasks) and convert them to a reasonable duration estimate (the amount of physical time on the calendar necessary to get the job done).

Now your next step is to quantify the actual tasks you need to accomplish.

Quantifying Tasks

Generally, the project's scope will contain only a handful of major deliverables. But each major deliverable may have several smaller deliverables that are significant as well. This is especially true for any scope items that will require several weeks or more to accomplish. If a major scope item requires only a week or two of effort, there probably aren't too many smaller scope items to be concerned with. If the task is large, like our 38-day estimate above, there's a good chance you can break that large task down into several smaller tasks to make them more manageable.

Remember: one bite at a time.

Assume that your large scope items are your project's milestones. Milestones are the key features or deliverables that your project owner expects to receive. Sometimes you have some negotiating options available to you where you can cut a milestone out of a project and choose to implement that specific portion at a later time. Breaking these scope items down into smaller chunks can make it a little easier to estimate.

If we go back to the 30,000-foot view, we're taking high-level items that basically just appear as large squares of color like our metaphoric agricultural fields, with no real definition to them (after all, can you really tell that the dark green field is corn, and the lighter green field is cabbage, when you're in an airplane?), and we're lowering ourselves down to a more practical height of about 5,000 feet, where it's a little easier to identify the specific tasks we're looking at. It's much easier to estimate the effort associated with moving a field of corn versus a field of cabbage when you can identify them as corn and cabbage.

Realistically, of course, you can't uproot and transplant entire crops, but I think you get the point. Narrowing down each major scope item into two to five smaller items gives you the opportunity to quantify the scope items a little better, and to do an accountability check on your estimates. Let's assume that your initial scope item that was estimated by your team member as requiring six to eight weeks to accomplish, can be broken down into three smaller tasks. When you present the individual items to them, they might estimate the first one will require one week of work, the second will require three weeks, and the third will require about two weeks. Now you have a slightly more accurate number: what was originally six to eight weeks as an estimate, was more accurately identified as closer to six weeks.

You have the option here, then, to either stick with the original estimate that was six to eight weeks, which you padded to be 72.5 days (which is about 14.5 weeks, given five business days per week), or you can reduce the effort estimate from the 75% you calculated as 38 days to the more accurate 30 days, and just recalculate your duration. As you get used to performing these steps, this will get easier over time, and your gut will be to either stick with your adjusted estimate, or to reassess.

Now the next step is to try to normalize your tasks as much as possible.

Normalizing Tasks

Normalizing tasks effectively means to try to reframe your individual tasks into a more standardized format that balances out each task relative to all other tasks.

In mathematics, normalizing is the act of multiplying by a factor that establishes a more normal balance of quantity. So, for each unit of time that you've assigned to the scope items, including the more detailed scope items you identified, try to get a slightly more accurate number.

If your overall project will take less than a month, you may want to express all of your estimates in hours. That way, if you had a scope item that was estimated at a week, but it had five sub-tasks within it, you can identify each sub-task as requiring about eight hours of work each. Assuming, of course, that each sub-task requires the same amount of time.

If your project will take more than a month, you may want to express everything in terms of days.

The end goal would be that you want to have as specific of an estimate as possible, so that when you recalculate your constants to determine the duration, and not just the effort estimate, you have something that's a little more specific.

Remember: estimates don't have to be accurate. They just have to be reasonable. They will get better over time.

Prioritizing Tasks

Defining priority for your tasks helps you to organize your project in a way that ensures that the scope items which are fundamentally defining to the project are given more attention than the items that are not. In normal development, code isn't always best written by following a sequence according to task priority, but rather according to similarity of function. You've probably heard, or said, the following phrase at some point in your development career: "Well, if we're in this area fixing this issue, we might as well fix these other issues in the same spot."

Because this tends to happen a lot, it doesn't always make sense to develop according to priority only. But it also doesn't make sense to ignore priority, otherwise you may end up delivering only a few features that are critical while missing many others. One of the best ways to determine priority is to sit down with your project's owners and stakeholders and go through the list of high-level scope items that were identified in the beginning. It may even be helpful to dive into the mid-level items that you determined in step three above, if the deliverables listed there will make sense to the project owners. If the deliverable is too technical for them, you may need to skip over those items, and just make the decisions within your technical team.

In this step, you just need to define whether the feature is foundational to the project or not. Don't be afraid to include the development priority as well. Your project owner may not be asking for you to build an Enterprise Service Bus to give them a messaging tool, but you might have determined that a service bus is the right way to do it, so you may elevate your own needs in the project to deliver the result they're asking for. Just don't lose sight of the business needs that they are defining. Here are a few questions you can ask to get those answers:

- Does this feature make or break the project?
- Would the project fail if we don't deliver this?

- Is this feature necessary the way it's defined, or is there an alternative way to implement this?
- Do we legitimately need to develop this feature, or is there an off-the-shelf product that will deliver it?

In the end, you are simply going to mark the scope item as being a priority item or not. You can just mark them with a star if they are.

Output

Now that you've completed this section, you should have a description of your preliminary scope, which is hopefully a relatively short and manageable list, and you should have a spreadsheet containing those scope items with some estimates beside them; both your baseline estimates, and your padded estimates for comparison.

Section 1.2: Qualifications

Inputs:

- Preliminary Scope document

Steps:

- Assess Importance
- Identify SMEs
- Identify Assumptions
- Identify Urgency
- Establish Deadlines
- Assign Workflow

Outputs:

- Preliminary Project and Task Estimates

Now that you've completed the basic estimating process, you should continue on to qualify as many of those estimates as you can. Remember that we are still in phase one of the process, before we've done any real project planning, so it's important to gather as much information to qualify your tasks as possible, so that your next phase of project planning can be more thorough. Since you've worked through a fairly high level of features and deliverables, and hopefully the list feels manageable, you'll want to look for any possible gaps or assumptions in the scope that might change the nature of what you're about to develop.

Project scope always needs to have a lot of clarity, because it's rarely correct from the initial round of estimates. When you look through your project's overall scope, try to ask yourself three questions about each scope item:

1. Where are we trying to be with this? Or, what is the primary goal of this scope item? The point is to identify the nature of what the project owner is expecting to accomplish with this item.
2. What's blocking us from accomplishing this? In some cases, it might be a simple answer: the only thing blocking us is that we have to build the solution. Maybe there are no barriers. Or, perhaps you need a significant infrastructure change, or a new server in place to build the solution. Whatever might be a potential barrier to accomplishing that result, identify it.
3. How do we lift that barrier? The easy answer can usually be a good answer, but not always the best answer. If you need a new server to solve a technical issue, it doesn't necessarily mean a $50,000 piece of hardware. A cloud-based virtual server might be sufficient; one you can discard when it's no longer needed.

Once you've gotten clarity on exactly what each scope item is trying to accomplish, your next priority is to identify the importance for all of the scope items.

Assessing Importance

To identify importance, you can use a method that divides the scope items according to their overall value. Each scope item and deliverable should fall into one of three categories, or, if you realize that they're just bad scope items that don't belong in the project at all, you can put them in a fourth category to defer those tasks to another project. The three main categories are:

- **Must Have's**: These are the scope items that are an absolute requirement for the project. These will usually be the starred items you selected above. Failing to deliver on these items would render the entire project a failure. There should be a compelling reason

44

why these were starred above, so you should document why to ensure it's kept as a priority during the development process. Knowing this will help the development process so that you can deliver according to needs.

- **Should Have's**: This is the default category for everything else that wasn't starred. You are effectively saying, "this feature should be a deliverable of this project; therefore, we will assume that it will be done." If there is a reason for a should-have item to be elevated to a must-have, document that and elevate it accordingly.

- **Nice-To-Have's**: These are the features that are optional but would still bring some value to the overall project. The value may be tangible or intangible, but they would be items that won't harm the project if they have to be cut from the first deployment. There should be a compelling reason to identify a scope item as being a nice-to-have instead of a should-have. If moving an item to the nice-to-have category won't break the project, it never hurts to do that, but you should keep in mind that while individual nice-to-have features may be expendable items in your project, the entire collective of nice-to-haves as a whole may not be. You may be able to cut one or more from the deliverables if needed, but if you ignore the entire nice-to-have category, you may end up delivering a project that isn't suitable to the project's owners.

Once you've separated the tasks into these three categories (or into a "deferred to another project" category), you need to rank them according to their priority sequence. If you follow the popular ABC prioritization method in your own task management work, you would be familiar with this process. Your three categories can be classified as categories A (must-have), B (should-have), and C (nice-to-have) respectively, and each deliverable within those categories will be ranked in order of importance or sequence.

This is a great time to pull out a spreadsheet and itemize your entire deliverable set. If you already did this when you were keeping track of your effort and duration estimates, you can add another column to identify the importance for the project owner. Have your project owner list the features from each category in the order of importance for them. If you get a response like "they're all important!" you can push back on this by picking two features and asking, "if you were only to get one of these features, which one would you prefer?" Sifting through the list with that mentality can reveal at least a few highly critical items that the owner simply couldn't live without, and the rest are slightly less important to them.

Let's use an example of a web application that provides a self-service portal for automotive services and appointment booking. The high-level T-estimate as the first data captured; the gut instinct of, "I think I can do this in about a week" or whatever estimate is appropriate. Using those T-estimates, in this example, we're normalizing according to hours, since this is a fairly small project. For large projects, you may wish to round to the nearest day, such that any scope items that are estimated to take less than a day (T1) are either rounded up to a day or are disregarded. In this case, the rounding is to the hour, so the normalized estimate shows the number of hours represented by the T-estimate. Using the same formulas as above, there is a padded estimate as well, which gives a rough idea of the duration, rather than just the effort required. The last column represents the importance to the project's owner, where A = must have, B = should have, and C = nice to have. This gives an immediate view into which items should be focused on first, regardless of whether you are planning as a waterfall project or whether each feature will be done in agile sprints.

	A	B	C	D	E	F
1	Project Scope Requests	T-Estimate	Normalized Estimate (hrs)	Padded Estimate (hrs)	Importance	
2	Account login functionality	3	40	76	A	
3	Vehicle history reports	2	8	15	C	
4	Service schedules	3	40	76	B	
5	Appointment calendar & booking	4	240	458	A	
6	Automotive care guides	2	8	15	C	
7	Live chat	2.5	20	38	B	
8	Cost calculator	3	40	76	C	
9						
10	Total Estimates		396	755		
11			Effort Estimate: 9.9 weeks	Duration Estimate: 18.9 weeks		

Identify Subject Matter Experts

Identifying your subject matter experts, or "SMEs" is a great way to diversify some decision-making, and to hold you and your team accountable to your development plan. Yielding decisions and recommendations to the SMEs is a good opportunity for them, relieves some of your pressure in managing the project, and helps to provide some validation when you need to get clarity on timelines and scope changes in the future.

If you don't have a team of SMEs available, this is a great time to refer to third-party expertise. You can reference other material from books, online sources, development agencies, and any other experts in your professional circles that can help to validate your plans. Wherever your source of SMEs comes from, make a point to identify them for each of the key areas of development, so that you know what sources to turn to when you run into challenges.

Identify Assumptions

One of the best tools you'll have at your disposal through your project is a full list of all of your starting assumptions. There are four great reasons why a list of assumptions is helpful to you:

1. It forces you to identify anything that needs to be proven before diving into the development process. Any assumptions that have high risks should be proven before moving ahead on the project. What if your project owner is assuming that if you add this new feature to your company's website, it will increase online sales by 50%, but they haven't done any studies to prove that? You might still be expected to deliver the result, but if you identify this upfront as an assumption, it's easier to call out that assumption later when you only get 1% growth, and a project owner tries to blame you for implementing it poorly.
2. It gives you a starting point to compare to so that if you have issues during the development process, you can refer back to an assumption to answer it. Why does this function always return a null value? Because initially, we assumed that the inputs would never be null, so we never handled null inputs properly.
3. It gives you a project variable that you can change later on in the project to help refine the result of the development.
4. It gives you a point of failure that you can point to when something breaks. If your project owners are aware of your assumptions going into the project, when something breaks as a result of the assumption being wrong, you can more easily justify time spent fixing an issue because you can use the assumption as the cause, without getting asked, "why didn't you think of that before you started?" This way, you can prove that you did.

Identify Urgency

While you already identified the sequence of importance with the project owners above, you may need to implement everything in a slightly different sequence when doing development, based on which tasks need to be done in which order to make them work correctly. You can't use an API in your application if you haven't built the API first. And you can't build the API unless you establish the API framework you're going to build on. Depending on your software architecture, it makes sense to build or deliver certain features in a specific order, regardless of their importance to the business. In development, we tend to reuse patterns, and coding a solution to solve one business need might also be the right solution for another, less important need. Combining the two into a single task might make it easier and faster to implement, since the development process will be focused on a single code-base to deliver both.

Don't be afraid to challenge your project owners and tell them that you'll be delivering features in a different order than they want, if there's a solid technical reason to do so. Generally, project owners are just looking for you to follow through on your commitments, rather than following a development sequence that doesn't make technical sense just because of the business priority. The trick, though, is to make sure you're selecting a sequence of deliverables that genuinely have a strong technical link to each other, rather than just a preference. This process is particularly important in agile development and development sprints, where features may be able to be deployed individually, rather than a waterfall approach where they all go at once.

Establish Deadlines

Deadlines can be great motivators, but they can also be a point of stress for developers and project managers. Project owners may try establishing deadlines based on nothing more than just a desire to have the project done, rather than on external factors that require that fixed time. It never hurts to challenge deadlines by asking questions. In fact, asking questions is probably the easiest and safest way to push back, although it can take a little finesse to word the question correctly.

When a project owner says, "this project needs to be done by September 1," you can always ask, "is there something happening in September that this project is tied to?" Or, when you estimate that a project is likely to take six months, and you're challenged with, "that's not good enough, we need it done in three months," you can ask whether it's based on some other factor that requires it to be completed by a specific date. By probing a little more deeply, you may find that many project owners don't have a specific reason other than their own personal urgency in wanting something completed.

Don't be afraid to challenge any of the deadlines you're given, so that you only need to identify realistic and required deadlines, rather than peoples' preferred dates. Conversely though, as a developer, and especially if you're managing a team of developers, you need to have some solid dates to hold your team to so that they can confidently and solidly deliver without feeling too much pressure, so there's a need to balance the pushback with your own willingness to just put in the effort. You still want some breathing room, but you don't want to have hard deadlines that aren't based on realistic expectations.

Assigning a Workflow

The last part of the assessment and estimating phase is to determine what development workflow you're likely to follow for the rest of the project. Most of the phases that I identify in this book are well suited to both agile and waterfall development, the latter of which is a more traditional approach, and in some cases, is the necessary approach when building an entirely new system or application for your company. Once a product is in place, however, additional development may follow either waterfall or various forms of agile processes.

This isn't a book about software development workflows, but it does speak to a few areas that are unique to waterfall or agile methodologies. For all intents, agile development isn't much different from waterfall development, except that instead of one giant waterfall, it's just lots of tiny little waterfalls with smaller, shorter deliverables. Agile does, however, have a larger mindset associated with its practices that can help to lift the rigid barriers that waterfall has on some projects. The process we've just gone through of identifying scope and getting clarity on every item can be implemented in either development workflow—you just need to implement smaller, simpler versions of each step for agile projects, and bigger, more detailed versions for waterfall ones.

At this point though, you should be able to make an educated enough decision about whether this project should be a full design, develop, deploy process (waterfall), or whether each of the core features can be delivered in smaller sprints (agile). Just because "agile" is a word that's used a lot in project management, doesn't mean it's always the best approach or that waterfall projects are bad. It depends on the type of project, the type of deliverables, and the nature of your organization's expectations.

If these two terms are relatively new to you, you can use the following general rules.

Your project should be run as a waterfall project if any of the following are true:

The project is less than about six weeks long. Since most agile sprints are about two weeks, you only get two to three basic releases in six weeks, which isn't much, nor is it too long to wait for three deliverables.

The project is a completely new system that is being built from scratch. If you have no pre-existing system to build on, you probably need a "big design up front" mentality before you have enough physical product to constitute a release.

Your project requires implementing a new major framework that you're not familiar with.

The requirements are well understood.

Your company isn't in the habit of making major changes during the process.

The project's outcome has limited risk, or minimal chance of a failure or cancelling that would result in excessive wasted code.

Your organization expects firm dates for the delivery. Agile has no issues with meeting dates inherently, but since you tend to implement a plan-build-deliver mentality repeatedly, there's a higher chance of missing a requirement without a full upfront plan.

Your project should be run as an agile project if any of the following are true:

There are lots of small deliverables.

The project builds on an existing system, augmenting its functionality.

The deliverables would be classified as "features" or "enhancements".

The project is largely a maintenance project.

The requirements are unclear or require validation.

Your project is subject to market conditions that might change.

When we reach additional sections shortly, I will identify areas where the process branches and has different implementations based on which development process you're following. For now, decide what methodology your project will need, and follow the next three phases according to that process.

Now that you've completed the Assessment and Estimating phase, it's a good idea to get final approval on your project with your project owners.

Knowing what project method applies helps in the approval process, because it sets the standard for your owners as to whether they are receiving a completed project at the end of a development process, or whether they can expect iterations and smaller deliverables over time.

Output

From this section, you should now have a more thorough spreadsheet containing a relatively accurate list of scope items, sufficient enough to qualify as a document that can be approved by your project owner, to affirm all of the core deliverables that you expect to produce in order to meet their requirements.

Chapter 5: Phase 2 - Planning and Architecture

"If you think good architecture is expensive, try bad architecture."
- Brian Foote

How can I build a realistic scope and project plan?

The first phase was all about understanding the business needs and requirements for your project, and seeking to get clarity on assumptions, details, people involved, and so forth. Assuming that your project owner is now tasking you with completing your software development project, it's time to start the Planning and Architecture phase.

The outcome of this entire phase is to take in the initial documentation you produced in phase one—the scope and effort estimates—and produce a proper business and project scope, a detailed project plan, and all of the necessary development requirements like use cases, models and processes, and architecture design.

As a kick-off for your project, you need to start with a solid brainstorming session.

Section 2.1: Brainstorming

Inputs:

- Preliminary Scope document and estimates

Steps:

- Initial Concepts
- Organization and Structure
- Gather Requirements

Outputs:

- List of Requirements

Brainstorming is something that you need to do with as many SMEs as possible, but don't go overboard. If you lead a large team, you may have multiple SMEs in the same area of discipline. You don't need them all, you usually just need one of them. Ideally, select the SMEs who will be doing the physical implementation on your project. If you lead a small team, or if you're the only developer, you can either do this process alone, or invite in others who are technically minded and can contribute to the development brainstorming process with you.

A good rule of thumb for brainstorming time is to spend about 10% of your project's overall time estimate in the brainstorming phase. For a week long project, that's about four hours. For a month-long project, it's about two days. For a year-long project, it may take close to six weeks. This is to cover all three of the steps below.

The purpose of brainstorming is to produce a complete list of requirements for your project.

Initial Concepts

Using the project's scope as a guideline, capture as many ideas about how to solve each scope requirement as possible. One of the most important rules about brainstorming is to prohibit anyone from raising any negative comments. Specifically, if someone suggests, "we can solve that scope item by using a Microsoft SQL Server, and SQL Server Reporting Services," this is not the time for your Linux guru to jump in and say, "MS SQL is terrible, just use Mongo DB and we can write our own reporting services." Don't let people shoot down any ideas for any reason. Every idea is worth capturing, and every contributor needs to be valued for their ideas. Not all will be kept, but they should always be considered.

A great brainstorming method is to capture each individual idea on a sticky note or whiteboard, or both. Using sticky notes makes it easy to move ideas around when they need to be organized.

Organization and Structure

Organizing your project's scope involves three steps when working with your brainstorm data.

First, separate out all of your brainstormed ideas according to the same criteria you used for prioritizing and defining the importance of your scope items in the Assessment and Estimating phase. Identify which brainstormed items are a must-have for the project, which are a should-have, and which are a nice-to-have. And once again, for any of the ideas that are not relevant or not practical for this project, move them into a fourth category for tracking elsewhere.

Second, for any ideas that are duplicate solutions, meaning that they solve the same item in different ways, identify which ones are the best option, which are second-best, third-best, and so on. Generally, you will only want to have one or two alternatives. These alternative solutions can come in handy later in the project if you run into a barrier that prevents a specific solution from working, and where an alternative solution is needed.

Third, match each of the ideas presented with the corresponding scope item that they solve, so that you can identify a critical path for your development. For each scope item, you'll have a defined solution, and backup solutions in the event that the preferred solution doesn't work.

Gather Requirements

The last step in the brainstorming section is to gather your requirements. This involves scanning through your list of scope items and the list of solutions you identified and making a list of any requirements you might have missed. This might be missed solutions, scope items that need to be added to the master scope list, or just base requirements that will resolve any assumptions you had outstanding from phase one.

If you need to add scope items to the master list, try to limit it to adding technical scope requirements within the business scope that was defined by your project owners. Adding to the business scope should generally only happen for the purpose of fulfilling an existing scope request, so it's good to keep them connected.

This full list of requirements will represent the following:

1. All the original scope items defined by the project owner.
2. All of the scope sub-items that were added in phase one when you broke down the major deliverables into smaller chunks. These will be sub-sections of the main scope items.
3. All of the additional mid- to low-level scope items that you added through this entire process, which will be grouped under the main scope items, or under the sub-sections.

In the end, you should have a three-tiered structure that represents all of the requirements for work effort that are needed for the project. Using the same spreadsheet example given previously, the following example shows the original scope items that were identified by the owner, the sub-items that are needed to accomplish it (in maximum two-week chunks as best as possible), and some mid-level items that would be used as clues and reminders during the development process. For instance, the REST/SOAP adapter under the CRUD API might still be further broken down into several individual tasks by the developer, if needed. This approach to drafting a list of requirements as to-do items will become the basis of the next section on Analysis.

	A	B	C	D	E	F
1	**Project Scope Requests**	**T-Estimate**	**Normalized Estimate (hrs)**		**Padded Estimate (hrs)**	**Importance**
2			**Breakdown Est. (h)**	**Summary Estimate**		
3	**Account login functionality**	3		40	76	A
4	Single Sign-on		8			
5	CRM Link		16			
6	Local DB and account		16			
7	**Vehicle history reports**	2		8	15	C
8	**Service schedules**	3		40	76	B
9	AutoBooker vehicle query		16			
10	AutoBooker calendar query		24			
11	**Appointment calendar & booking**	4		250	477	A
12	CRUD API for AutoBooker		80			
13	REST/SOAP adapter					
14	JSON endpoint					
15	Exchange calendar API link		40			
16	AutoBooker calendar API link		40			
17	Javascript calendar plugin		50			
18	Link to SMS notification system		40			
19	**Automotive care guides**	2		8	15	C
20	**Live chat**	2.5		20	38	B
21	API Link to phone chat API		12			
22	Web link to API		8			
23	**Cost calculator**	3		40	76	C
24	API query to AutoBooker		8			
25	Calculator Javascript UI		32			
26						
27	Total Estimates			406	774	
28				*Effort Estimate: 10.15 weeks*	*Duration Estimate: 19.3 weeks*	

Output

This thorough list of requirements is a draft project scope definition, which should be enough to define a completed business scope, and to perform any proof-of-concept work that is needed before finalizing the plan.

Section 2.2: Analysis

Inputs:

- List of Requirements

Steps:

- Develop Business Scope and Charter
- Proof of Concept
- Validate Requirements
- Develop Project Scope
- Establish Budget and Timeline Constraints
- Define Project Plan

Outputs:

- Business Scope / Charter
- Project Scope
- Project Plan

This is probably the most important section of the entire set of project phases. The end of this section will determine whether you will be moving ahead with the project or not. In this book, I'm covering only the high-level expectations for this section, but stay tuned for some future material, where I'll be going through the planning and architecture phase in more detail, outlining exact steps, and providing real-world examples.

For now, let's just look at the most important path of this part of the process.

Develop Business Scope and Charter

For many projects in smaller organizations, the business scope and charter is a fairly straightforward document. For projects that are up to only a few months long, this document only needs to be a single page. The purpose of a business scope or a business charter is to outline the primary goals and outcomes expected for a project and to identify the communication strategy on how you as the project manager will provide updates on the progress of your project to the owners and stakeholders. Note that a business scope differs from a project scope, in that the business scope deals with business-level deliverables rather than software deliverables. Depending on how detailed the original project scope was, this might just be a re-representation of the same scope items but presented in a more business-oriented manner. In essence, an executive summary.

Some companies will expect a charter to include budget and timeline constraints. We will be identifying those a little later on so you can always come back to your charter and add them in once they're completed.

Proof of Concept

Undoubtedly there will be several assumptions you made in phase one or there will be requirements that you gathered in the brainstorming section which require a proof of concept before proceeding with development. The proof of concept does not always mean that you are proving whether or not something *can* be done, but rather to implement a sample that provides a guideline to your developers, even if it's just to yourself, that gives an indication of *how* it should be done so that you are able to do a full implementation later on in the coding process.

Validate Requirements

Similar to a proof of concept you now want to validate any of the requirements that you previously identified. This doesn't need to be overly complicated and can simply be a checklist of affirmations where you confirm that the requirement is possible, achievable, and reasonable as a solution for the scope item you were trying to solve. For all intents, this is just a process of crossing your Ts and dotting your Is to confirm that the requirements can be completed.

Develop the Project Scope

In my experience many developers who build applications or solutions in smaller companies have a desire to just jump into coding right off the bat. For those who are a little more disciplined, they will define a rudimentary project plan outlining some of the requirements or tasks that need to be done, especially if a project plan is expected by their project owners or other management or executives within a company.

The project scope is a more detailed version of the original scope that was identified. The project scope needs to include any additional proof of concept items, requirements, or identified solutions that are needed in order to accomplish the project. The first scope identified the business outcomes that the organization is looking for. The project scope includes both the business outcomes and the technical outcomes that are necessary in order to complete this. This is particularly important if you have significant implementation requirements that have large budget, time, or resource impacts which need to be identified.

If you are dependent on other teams to get the job done, or if you need to buy new hardware or software, or implement new technological solutions, it's good to call all of these things out upfront and before the project begins. For all intents you are taking the business scope and adding in the technical scope. It doesn't have to identify every individual task, since we will cover that in the project plan shortly, but it does need to identify the high- and mid-level technical deliverables that are necessary to accomplish the business outcomes.

Establish Budget and Timeline Constraints

By this time you will have enough information to identify any additional budget requests that you need to account for, and if, in the process of gathering all of this information you have also received a hint from the organization as to when they expect this project to be done, then you probably have a good idea of any timeline constraints that you should account for as well.

For any budget information, you should keep track of this in a separate spreadsheet so that you can submit budget requests in accordance with your organization's budget practices. This probably means identifying fixed, upfront costs first, and whether or not there are any ongoing maintenance or SLA costs associated with those purchases. If you are leasing any solutions or implementing anything that requires recurring costs such as monthly fees those should be identified as well.

You now have all of the information that you need to develop a full and complete project plan.

Define the Project Plan

As you can probably imagine, this would be the most complicated and time-consuming part of the process if we had not already done the majority of the work in the previous sections. Everything we have done to date has been for the sole purpose of building this project plan, and it has simply been a walk-through using an iterative process to complete this.

The effort associated with identifying scope, quantifying and normalizing tasks, assessing importance, identifying assumptions, and identifying the urgency of each task as well as gathering any additional requirements leads us to this point where we define the basic project plan. While this step may take many days or weeks without the preceding information, the iterative approach that we have taken thus far makes this a simple step.

If your company uses project management software of any kind, this is a great time to make use of it. If you don't have any formal project management software, you can track this kind of information either in a basic task manager that allows you to create subtasks—because it's important to be able to maintain a hierarchy of tasks grouped under the core scope—or even using software such as Microsoft Excel to keep a list of tasks and their current status in columns. Use whatever method works best for you.

Your first level of tasks should be the primary scope that was identified in phase one. Indented below each of those scope items would be any of the subtasks or additional scope items that you added since that time in order to accomplish the primary scope. From there you can either add more second-level items, or indent further to a third level, providing a complete list of all of the major deliverables that are needed for your development team. Each developer that is working on the project may then further break down any of those tasks into smaller, individual tasks, especially if they need to identify specific functions or classes, or specific types of solutions that need to be built in order to accomplish the desired result. Unless you are the only developer you shouldn't need to break the tasks down to that granular of a level since you can just leave that up to each developer to manage on their own.

It doesn't hurt to include as many low-level task estimates as you can because once you identify every individual requirement you may wind up reassessing the time estimates that you put to the larger scope items and may determine a slightly more realistic number. If this is the case, don't be afraid to go back and refine the estimates that you originally put in place. The spreadsheet where you outlined the scope items and their estimates initially can now be retired as you will transfer all of that information into your new project scope.

The following is an example of the same spreadsheet demo we used above but represented in project management software that provides a similar visual style. This particular application, OmniPlan, also displays a Gantt-style timeline with relative times indicating the effort and duration estimates. The overall project plan is estimated to require about 10 weeks of effort, spread over about 19 weeks in duration.

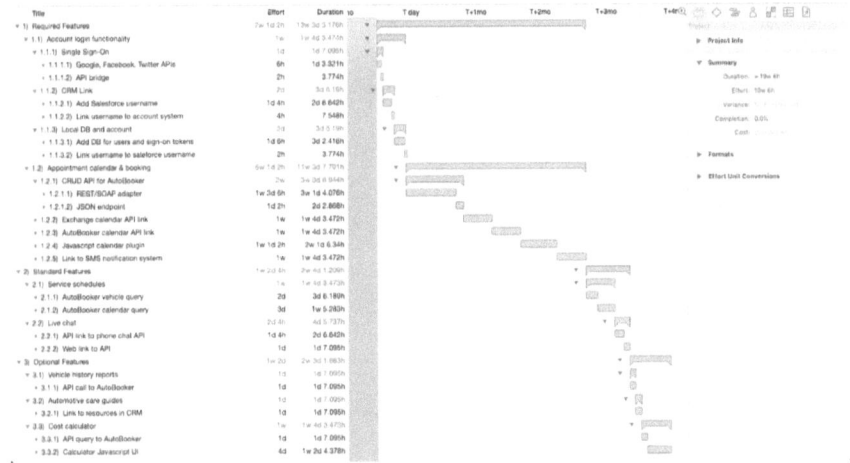

Looking a little closer, you can see how the plan closely mirrors the example in a spreadsheet, as well as how the project summary can provide a comparison between effort and duration:

Title	Effort	Duration
▼ 1) Required Features	7w 1d 2h	13w 3d 3.176h
▼ 1.1) Account login functionality	1w	1w 4d 3.474h
▼ 1.1.1) Single Sign-On	1d	1d 7.095h
• 1.1.1.1) Google, Facebook, Twitter APIs	6h	1d 3.321h
• 1.1.1.2) API bridge	2h	3.774h
▼ 1.1.2) CRM Link	2d	3d 6.19h
• 1.1.2.1) Add Salesforce username	1d 4h	2d 6.642h
• 1.1.2.2) Link username to account system	4h	7.548h
▼ 1.1.3) Local DB and account	2d	3d 6.19h
• 1.1.3.1) Add DB for users and sign-on tokens	1d 6h	3d 2.416h
• 1.1.3.2) Link username to saleforce username	2h	3.774h
▼ 1.2) Appointment calendar & booking	6w 1d 2h	11w 3d 7.701h
▼ 1.2.1) CRUD API for AutoBooker	2w	3w 3d 6.944h
• 1.2.1.1) REST/SOAP adapter	1w 3d 6h	3w 1d 4.076h
• 1.2.1.2) JSON endpoint	1d 2h	2d 2.868h
• 1.2.2) Exchange calendar API link	1w	1w 4d 3.472h
• 1.2.3) AutoBooker calendar API link	1w	1w 4d 3.472h
• 1.2.4) Javascript calendar plugin	1w 1d 2h	2w 1d 6.34h
• 1.2.5) Link to SMS notification system	1w	1w 4d 3.472h
▼ 2) Standard Features	1w 2d 4h	2w 4d 1.209h
▼ 2.1) Service schedules	1w	1w 4d 3.473h
• 2.1.1) AutoBooker vehicle query	2d	3d 6.189h
• 2.1.2) AutoBooker calendar query	3d	1w 5.283h
▼ 2.2) Live chat	2d 4h	4d 5.737h
• 2.2.1) API link to phone chat API	1d 4h	2d 6.642h
• 2.2.2) Web link to API	1d	1d 7.095h
▼ 3) Optional Features	1w 2d	2w 3d 1.663h
▼ 3.1) Vehicle history reports	1d	1d 7.095h
• 3.1.1) API call to AutoBooker	1d	1d 7.095h
▼ 3.2) Automotive care guides	1d	1d 7.095h
• 3.2.1) Link to resources in CRM	1d	1d 7.095h
▼ 3.3) Cost calculator	1w	1w 4d 3.473h
• 3.3.1) API query to AutoBooker	1d	1d 7.095h
• 3.3.2) Calculator Javascript UI	4d	1w 2d 4.378h

▼ Summary

Duration: > 19w 6h

Effort: 10w 6h

Variance: No Baseline Set

Completion: 0.0%

Cost: Unspecified

In this particular application, one of the ways to calculate the estimate padding we accounted for previously is to set the efficiency factor of the resources that are assigned to the tasks. Using the three padding values of 22% slack, 25% inaccuracy, and 25% BAU, we can determine the following approximate efficiency percentage:

```
= ((1 + 22%) + 25%) + 25%
= (1.22 + 25%) + 25%
= 1.525 + 25%
= 1.91
```

I'm just showing the steps here to avoid any confusion about the compounding. The result means that every unit of time, in this example, should be padded by about 91%, or 191% of the estimated value. To reverse engineer that as a "factor of inefficiency" we need the inverse of 91%: $1 \div 1.91 = 0.52$. So, our resources work at about 52% capacity in order to determine a duration estimate. By setting the resources to be 52% efficient, the effort estimate remains intact, as you can see in the effort column in the diagram, while the duration is padded to compensate. This is a particularly helpful technique if you have different efficiency factors for different resources, as the software will adjust accordingly depending on which resources are assigned to which tasks.

If you're able to build a simple project list and transfer your estimates and your efficiency factor to a project management tool, you'll have output similar to the above. If you don't have any project management software, most of the same calculations can be done using a spreadsheet, although you may wish to take advantage of some formulas and calculations to get your estimates. Either way, this is all that's necessary to give your team the necessary marching orders for the project.

Output

Congratulations! You have successfully created a project plan! Everything you do from this point forward will use the business scope and charter (as a guideline) and a combination of the project scope and the project plan to see it through to completion.

If your organization requires some kind of approval before moving ahead with the design and development of your software, you should now have enough information to get that approval. This is particularly valuable for getting budget and timeline buy-in.

* * *

This is also a spot to pause for a moment and identify our first critical path split. By this point, you have done all of the initial work for a basic project, and you have a working plan with feature-focused deliverables, and a realistically achievable timeline. From now on, your project may have different implementation methods based on your workflow.

If you are doing a waterfall project, you will most likely work through each of the remaining sections in sequence, completing each section before moving on to the next. If you are doing an agile project, you will apply the next seven sections in an iterative approach, repeating all seven sections for each major feature or deliverable. Depending on the size of the feature, you may also iterate through smaller releases that can be built, tested, and deployed before eventually delivering the milestone feature.

In either case, the same timing and implementation I identified at the start of phase two applies. Initial design should consume about one-ninth (as a rough guideline) of the overall remaining time, development will consume about one-third, and testing will consume another third.

Section 2.3: Design

Inputs:

- Project Scope

Steps:

- Establish Business Use Cases
- Define Development Parameters
- Define Tests and Scenarios
- Develop Conceptual Models
- Define Business Processes
- Develop Interface Wireframes
- Validate Design Concepts

Outputs:

- Use Cases
- Models and Processes
- Architecture

For some developers, architecture comes naturally to them. For others, this can be a difficult process. In another book I plan to cover how to handle architectural design if you, as a developer have never done software architecture before. For now, I'm going to skim through the design phase and cover just the basics.

Waterfall: spend the full time planning the entire design of the system but be careful not to over-engineer the architecture such that it becomes monolithic. Try to think of the shortest path to implementation while maintaining the integrity that your system needs.

Agile: focus primarily on this specific sprint's design needs, but don't lose sight of the overall system's requirements so that your design doesn't need to be changed multiple times. Keep the full scope of the business requirements in your mind as you continue to design.

If you are building a web application, many aspects of the design phase may be handled by graphic designers or members of your marketing team. Since many web architectures are relatively standard, there tends to be less application architecture design, and a little more back-end architecture, so you'll end up sharing the design workload between visual design for the application's user experience, and architectural design for the application's operation. Since you are likely managing the project from a developer's perspective, most of my focus will be on the architectural design elements, but for a visually heavy application, you will apply some of these same concepts to visual design as well.

Unlike several years ago when design and development were mutually exclusive, the two disciplines are now quite closely connected. In web application development some might argue that the design is just as much a development discipline as it is a marketing and graphics discipline. After all, a good designer needs to have a solid understanding of CSS, HTML, JavaScript, source control and extensive testing practices.

Focusing more on the application design, this phase will require a little bit of diagramming expertise and being able to identify how an application should work in a visual flow, beginning with use cases. I won't cover details on how to do this diagramming, as you can easily search online for videos or tutorials on how to do specific diagrams. Instead, I will be focusing on the reasons why these kinds of diagrams are helpful, rather than walking you through the process of doing them.

Before moving into this section, it's important to resist the natural developer urge to just start coding. In the same way that moving through the planning sections step by step made it easier to establish a solid, easy project plan, working through this design section thoroughly will make it easier to implement the coding requirements later. Resist the urge! You'll thank me later.

Establish Business Use Cases

In this phase your architects and developers will define use cases in accordance with the business requirements. For each major scope item identified at the beginning the most helpful way to build a solid use case, if you've never done this before, is to treat each business function the same way you treat a software function.

A typical software function will take in zero or more inputs and will usually produce one or more outputs. Usually the function performs some kind of translation on the inputs in order to create the outputs. A function that does not take in any inputs directly usually still produces outputs that are based on assumptions or fixed data instead of an input. A UUID generator, for example, may not take in any inputs, but would generate a standard format UUID based on a precondition or assumption that you want a 36-character string composed of hexadecimal numbers and hyphens in a specific format.

While you may never need to break down this type of a function into the details required in a use case, the concept still applies on how business functions should also work. Any general business function should have a primary purpose of taking in some data, manipulating that data in some form, and producing some kind of output. So, when you are looking through your scope items where your project owner has identified a deliverable, you should already know what is required in order to create that solution, a general idea of how to accomplish it, and some kind of expectation on what should be produced at the end. If you're not familiar with building use cases, you don't need to overcomplicate it. Just do a web image search so that you can get a visual on what they look like and use that as a guideline to identify what parts of the system need to accomplish what tasks in order to achieve the desired outcome. This may involve some sequence of tasks that move from your application's UI to its program logic to its business logic, to your datastore, and back up through the UI to produce a result.

If the idea of a diagram is paralyzing to you, you can always represent the process in a textual fashion by using a sequence of steps in a numbered list, and a few basic if..then statements to identify the control flow.

Define Development Parameters

This is a fairly basic step, where architects and developers establish the specific inputs and outputs of business use cases to ensure appropriate data is functional in the development cycle. The goal is to convert business inputs and outputs to programmatic inputs and outputs. This can be represented using just a basic text-based use case, or you can use a UML Class Diagram to identify inputs and outputs.

For instance, if the business use case says to take in the customer's address and return back the GPS coordinates of their home, you might identify the development parameters as each individual field: the street address, city, province or state, and country, and that you'll return back a latitude and longitude value as a string.

Or you may have a business use case that starts with capturing personal information from a customer, putting that information into your organization's CRM, and then responding back with a confirmation of the updated information. For development parameters, you want to establish the development use cases which will list specific input and output requirements, identifying exact data types and expected formats.

This is a time where it's important to be detail-oriented. Translating business requests into explicit development requests can wind up with a lot of assumptions if it's not done correctly. Does your function that needs to take in a text value need to restrict input to 50 characters, 255 characters, or a 4 GB text blob? Knowing this can significantly impact the architectural design process, and whether something like a text field on a web page is sufficient for input, or whether a file upload with document conversion is the more accurate requirement.

For API development, this is a great time to start thinking about the API method architecture so that you start planning some of the method and package names that your API will use.

Define Tests and Scenarios

Sadly, this is one of the areas where many developers start to laugh a bit what I tell them that they need to define their tests upfront. Almost everyone knows that as a general rule of thumb this is a good practice, but in organizations that do not have heavy software development lifecycle implementations, this may be a luxury that developers can't afford. This is a good time to do some preplanning and to establish at least a few basic test patterns and possible conditions that could occur in the development process so that your developers have some kind of guideline on how to test whether or not their function works.

But even if you aren't able to define specific tests and conditions, this is a great time to make sure that you have testing and staging environments in place so that you can test whether the software you develop will dynamically adapt to different environments when deployed. The last thing you want to do is to get your software working in a single test environment and then find out that you have to rewrite a chunk of your code when you try to deploy it to a production environment. Setting up your test and staging environments right at the beginning helps to ensure that you develop with environmental considerations in mind.

Develop Conceptual Models

Conceptual models are programmatic representations of either data models or operational components. These can be expressed as either text descriptions, or you may wish to use a more detailed UML class diagram.

Particularly if you are developing an object-oriented solution, this is your opportunity to draft basic functional classes with non-operational methods built in so that you can get a feel for the overall organization of your software solution. This can include abstract classes and interfaces to help build some initial concepts.

For functional programming, it's a good time to plan some of the high-level structural requirements, assuming you're not using an existing software framework that will define that structure for you.

For data-driven applications this may be a good time to define some of your core data models, assuming you need to build some.

Define Business Processes

This is one of the trickier parts in the design phase. Most of the basic business processes should already be defined in the business use cases, especially if each use case represents the majority of the process. Some processes may be more complex and require combinations of one or more use cases to accomplish a bigger result. You should use your business use cases as a guideline and work with your architects and/or developers to define some step-by-step requirements for specific coding deliverables and establish any critical operational logic that is necessary for your business requirements. You don't need to break this down function by function, but at least at a mid-level, you should establish a sequence of operational steps that are necessary to create a functional operation in code that will accomplish the desired outcome.

The overall outcome you should expect at this phase is to be able to define all of the logic validators that are necessary to confirm that your business logic is solid, and that you know what needs to be developed, from a coding perspective, to get results.

This is also an excellent time to validate and affirm your use cases, as your interconnected processes will help to identify whether the outputs from a specific use case match the input requirements for another use case when the functions are chained together in a larger process.

Using a BPMN business process diagram can be particularly helpful here, as these are the kinds of diagrams that can be easily understood by non-technical users and can be used to communicate overall processes to your project owners. Individual development use cases and models aren't as valuable to executive team members, but BPMN is a fairly standard methodology that you can use to present well, or at the very least, shame your managers if they're not familiar with it. I mean "educate." Educate your managers.

Develop Interface Wireframes

If your application has a heavy UI or UX component, this is the time to establish the interface wireframes that are necessary to provide end-users with an easy way to control the business logic of your application. While your graphic and user interface design teams should be part of this process right from the beginning so that they have insight into the project, the actual act of creating interface wireframes should not begin until after all of the business processes have been defined. This adheres to the "form follows function" concept, in that design should begin only when the functional aspects of the system are defined. The interfaces should follow the functional requirements, not the other way around.

If you have an application that is not UI-heavy, like a public API, you can still design a type of interface wireframe by establishing any necessary patterns for your API that will give some kind of visual insight into how it works. This may be a workflow diagram, examples of API data output, network diagrams, or other similar models that provide visuals on the structure of your application.

Validate Design Concepts

This is the simplest part of the design phase. All of the people responsible for the design and development aspects of your project get together and review all of the previously prepared documents—the project plan, use cases, development parameters, conceptual models, business processes, and wireframes—to confirm them for accuracy and feasibility in development. Any alterations or corrections that need to be done before development begins should happen now.

Output

At this point, you should have a full stack of text descriptions, use cases, and diagrams representing your entire project's overall architecture, along with any visual or structural models to qualify as a full architecture for your project. Make sure that you keep these diagrams in an easily accessible location and name the files appropriately so that they can be retrieved and viewed by your staff. Using a web-based file sharing service like Dropbox, or other system that can show thumbnails as a browsing method can be helpful, because most developers won't have any idea what your `112.113-Arch-NoArg-UserDiag-BPMN-V-8.1.473-R3-Final-Draft2.jpg` file is, unless they can see the thumbnail and know right away that it's the diagram for your login process.

Seriously, architects, stop naming files like this.

Make these files accessible, visible, easy to search for, and wherever possible, include any tags or other descriptors that will make it easy for another developer to find the file they need by just typing in the word "login" or by clicking on a tag to filter the list. When you're working on a multi-year international project, trust me, you need this.

Chapter 6: Phase 3 - Development

"Without requirements or design, programming is the art of adding bugs to an empty text file."
- Louis Srygley

As a developer, the last thing you need to read is a tutorial on how to do development, so this chapter will be focused more on the issues that a developer faces during the project lifecycle related to project management specifically, as you work through your development phase.

There are three areas where developers regularly have project management challenges when their mind is focused on coding:

- **Organizing Architecture:** aligning architecture to development in an organized manner
- **Building and Coding:** staying on track with the building and coding process even when scope changes
- **Reviewing and Testing:** performing good code reviews and tests without causing more scope changes

Let's start with the first issue: translating architecture to code while staying organized.

Section 3.1: Organizing Architecture

Inputs:

- Architecture
- Project Plan

Steps:

- Define and Document Core Architecture
- Establish File and Code Structures
- Define Development Templates and Patterns
- Design Class and Object Structures

Outputs:

- Implementation Architecture
- Templates and Patterns
- Pseudocode
- Developer Documentation

The above steps for development architecture are relatively standard expectations in software projects, but the steps indicated here have more value from a project management perspective.

I firmly believe that the single most valuable skill in learning to master the art of translating architecture to code is to perfect your documentation. Like any other skill, you only master it by practicing it, so it's important to just document everything you can. If you're already excellent at documentation, translating architecture to code will be easier for you. But for most of the developers I know, documentation has been that necessary evil that is only done because someone demands it, when what they really want to do is spend their time coding. When following a good architecture though, documentation can be just as enjoyable as coding, especially when you look back six months later and thank yourself for keeping the documentation clear. Good documentation will save your life! Or at least your project, anyway.

Spend time reviewing architecture patterns and using them as a guideline to identify which deliverables are dependent on which patterns. This will help you and your team to confirm that your code is aligned with the architecture, and that you're keeping track of any documentation needs for reporting at a project management level. Your team needs to understand the value of writing code that meets the architectural requirements, and to do that, they need to report to you regularly on the deliverables. When you first established the list of to-do items, you left the specific task details up to the developer to implement. This can result in the developer—even if it's you—focusing so much on the code that they forget to connect the code back to the requirements on the project. Keep the two constantly connected—code and requirements—and regularly report on the high-level task items that are business-focused. This way, you are keeping an eye on how the code implementation is meeting the critical business needs.

You also need to regularly encourage your developers to keep you informed as they progress in their work. If you've estimated that a specific deliverable is going to take five days to accomplish, and you've broken that down into twenty smaller tasks, then you can reasonably assume that every day will see four of those tasks completed. That means that by the second day, you should have a good view into whether the five-day estimate is going to be accomplished or not, and that gives you enough time to make adjustments if needed, before the deadline hits. This kind of tracking and insight means committing to even a basic project management software solution that allows you to check on the status of a task, so that you can relate that back up to the higher-level items. Ensure that your developers keep a good record of their time and activity as they work through those items, especially if you can match their work hours to the actual time spent on the deliverables, so that you can relate that to the estimates you had at the beginning. Don't be afraid to check in regularly, especially on the first projects you and your team work on, when following this methodology. Using some kind of project management tool allows you to check in a little more passively, so that your team doesn't feel like you're constantly looking over their shoulders.

Keeping yourself and your developers well organized and communicating regularly helps to ensure you're always keeping an eye on the progress.

Output

The result of this section is to produce the first draft of code that you need to finalize the rest of your development process. This will include as much documentation as is necessary to start filling in the blanks to complete the full scope of development work. Part of the advantage to having this draft implementation in place is to allow different teams to be able to build their sections without waiting on too many deliverables from other teams. For a more detailed description of what this looks like in practice, I'll cover this in more depth in the next section.

Section 3.2: Building / Coding

Inputs:

- Developer Documentation

Steps:

- Develop Logic Flows and Functional Sequences
- Develop Functional Implementation
- Build Unit and Functional Tests and Scenarios

Outputs:

- Code
- Testing Environments

The three development steps listed above for this section are a more iterative approach to development, which can be helpful when addressing project scope changes. Scope change is a common project management issue that you're likely to face when working through a project in an organization that doesn't have development as its primary business. Scope changes can happen unexpectedly and uncontrollably, and if they are not managed well, they can be some of the most stressful conditions. You may be expected to deliver on time and on budget, even when your project owner has added fifty percent more work to your to-do list! So how can you keep the programming on track when scope changes?

First, recognize that scope change is mostly inevitable. We refer to it as scope creep, because the change usually creeps up on us without warning, and it can be stressful trying to learn how to adapt to that kind of change. The key to handling it well is to start with the assumption that it's going to happen, and plan for the possibility that you will need to pause and shift your deliverables accordingly. A great way to do this is to treat each of your high-level deliverables as independent items, with an expectation that at any point in time, the project could simply stop, and you may still want to deliver on the work done to date. Being prepared for the worst possible scenario makes it easier to adapt to other changes as they happen.

In a software development company, this kind of project halt is a little less common, since most if not all of the people involved in the project have a deeper understanding of the development process and are more committed to software-oriented results. But in a non-development organization, project stakeholders generally have little to no understanding of the impact that a decision-change has on the development lifecycle and are simply looking for non-development related business deliverables.

While I won't cover the details of how to account for major course corrections—that's a topic for another book—there are a few tips I recommend that can help developers minimize the amount of code refactoring that's needed when basic scope changes occur.

Scope Change Mitigation Tip #1: Use Iterative Development

One of the typical impacts of a scope change is that an existing solution is in a half-completed state when the requirements shift, and this can result in unexpected code issues, as entire sections of code are often incomplete before the change happened. Rolling back half-changes or removing entire sections of code tends to cause more issues, and even if you were perfect in your source control by committing every functional code change, it can often be more work to undo what you've done than it is to just finish it anyway. Taking an iterative approach in implementation can help with this, as it makes it easier to separate complete code from incomplete code. To do this, start by writing perfect code as a draft. I can imagine that you're thinking, "yeah, right," because I basically just said, "avoid code issues by being perfect." What I mean by "perfect code" is not necessarily error-free, or bug-free code, it's code that will work and operate in a perfect condition, and return a perfect result, even though that's not a real-world behavior. For your first iteration, write your functions under the assumption that you will not be receiving any bad data as an input, that your data sources will be available and will return exactly the data you need, and that you will generate perfect output to return from your function. For example:

```
// Iteration 1
// Java function declaration with defined input,
// output, and a perfect return value

/**
```

```
 * Gets the customer's city name from the CRM.
 *
 * @param  customerId  the customer id in the format 1-
23456-789
 * @return             the customer's city name
 * @throws Exception   if anything happens
 */
public String getCustomerCity(String customerId) throws
Exception {
return "Tokyo";
}
```

This is fully functional, and fully documented, but it assumes that the environment is perfect. There is no data validation, no error handling, and the returned result is fictitious. But this code will compile, and deploy in a testing environment without issues, and only takes about two minutes to write.

For the second iteration, refine your code by returning valid results and accounting for realistic errors. Bad input data, offline data sources, missing write permissions when saving your results, that kind of thing. For example:

```
// Iteration 2
// Java function revised with realistic data and basic
errors
/**
 * Gets the customer's city name from the CRM.
 *
 * @param  customerId  the customer id in the format 1-
23456-789
 * @return             the customer's city name
 * @throws CrmException            If CRM is offline
 * @throws DataNotFoundException   If no city on file
 * @throws ValidatorException      If id is invalid
 */
public String getCustomerCity(String customerId) throws
CrmException, ValidatorException, DataNotFoundException {

if (! Validator.isCustomerId(customerId)) {
throw new ValidatorException("Customer id is invalid.");
}
return CrmApi.getCustomerInfo(customerId, "city");
}
```

In this example, the Validator object may throw a CrmException, or it may return false if the number isn't in the system. This now adds the proper exception handlers and should now trigger code requirements to update any calling functions to ensure that exceptions are handled properly.

Then, for your last iteration, refine the code by accounting for all of the edge cases you can think of. Completely wrong data types, missing entire sets of data, getting back a million results from a query when you're expecting to get a maximum of five, and so forth.

```java
// Iteration 3
// Java function revised with edge case errors
/**
 * Gets the customer's city name from the CRM.
 *
 * @param  customerId  the customer id in the format 1-
23456-789
 * @return             the customer's city name
 * @throws CrmException           If CRM is offline
 * @throws DataNotFoundException  If no city on file
 * @throws NullException          If id is null
 * @throws ValidatorException     If id is invalid
 */
public String getCustomerCity(String customerId) throws
CrmException, ValidatorException, NullException,
DataNotFoundException {
if (customerId == null) {
throw new NullException("Customer id is null");
}
if (! Validator.isCustomerId(customerId)) {
throw new ValidatorException("Customer id is invalid.");
}
return CrmApi.getCustomerInfo(customerId, "city");
}
```

This allows you to keep using and testing your builds without breaking anything, which lets other developers on your team continue their work, even when you aren't done yours, and without unnecessary merge conflicts. If you're the only developer, it also lets you define your entire application's code structure so that you can begin implementation, demos, and user acceptance tests long before the code is complete.

This particular methodology is especially valuable in API development, when functions may need to be available for testing even if the results aren't perfectly captured from your data sources.

By working through development iteratively like this, if a scope change occurs half way through, you can easily determine which functions are no longer needed, and which need to be refined, and there's far less work in making the change, because you have a draft of all your functions in place. If you instead tried to perfect each function as you go, you may end up throwing away a lot of work, and then working harder to complete new functions that you hadn't yet started. Throwing away draft code that isn't refined is much less discouraging than throwing away near-complete solutions.

Scope Change Mitigation Tip #2: Review Daily

As a project manager, it's a good idea to check in on the status of your project daily. You don't need to devote hours of time to this, but rather just spot-checks on critical items. When you're the only developer, and you're trying to handle the project management as well, having this high-level check-in on your own work helps to keep yourself accountable to the timeline, when your head is otherwise naturally drawn to focusing on the code.

One frequent developer mistake that I've seen when it comes to coordination with a project manager, is getting too buried in the process of writing code and forgetting to check in with the manager on whether that code is aligning with the project's expectations. It's common for developers to try to solve the problem within the problem, recursively, and eventually lose sight of the objective they were working towards in the first place. Using the iterative approach above helps to prevent that because it forces a review of semi-functional code before it's completed but after it's in a functional state.

You should be reviewing your project plan at least once a week in its entirety, but still checking in daily to stay organized and to make sure that your development patterns are on track.

Scope Change Mitigation Tip #3: Communicate Early, Communicate Often

You need to expect, and require, open communication among your team. As part of your daily check-in on the project, make a point to identify any issues that require discussion, whether it's between you and your development team, or between you and your project stakeholders. Make sure your developers are accumulating questions or clarifications that they need and are submitting them to you daily. If it can't be daily, then at least twice a week, especially for projects that are only a month or two in length. Using the iterative approach can raise several questions early on that provide clarity to complete the additional iterations. What kind of data can we expect as an input? How many results will the user expect to get back from this type of request? How will we handle data that isn't conforming to expectations before we run it through an adapter to put it in our CRM, ERP, or CMS? These are the kinds of questions that come up in iterative processes and should be raised with you quickly.

Passing the question over to the people that can answer them, while continuing to develop solutions iteratively—making the assumption that the function should run perfectly first, with details filled in later—gives you time to get answers without stalling the development process. This also means that you can accumulate questions during the day, pass them on to the experts, and use your daily check-in time the next morning to communicate the answers back to your team so that development can account for those answers when they move on to their next iteration.

Scope Change Mitigation Tip #4: Use the Three-Times Rule as a Gut Check

One of the most valuable tips I've offered to developers for checking in on a task and ensuring it's staying on track is to regularly review the estimates and the scheduled deadline on a task, and use what I call a "three-times" rule as a guideline for checking in. Here's how the three-times rule works: however much time you estimated for a task, you should multiply that by three, and check in at least that much earlier than when the task is due.

When you set up your project initially, you should have high-level estimates of how long each task should take. When you further break down those tasks into individual items, you also have a good idea of the length of time required for each of them. This means that most of your estimates will have at least some kind of broad guess about the time required to complete it that should be reasonably accurate.

Let's say, for instance, that you have a milestone deliverable on a project, such as, "allow customers to edit their full profile on their account." You've estimated that to implement this entire task, it will take ten days of work. Then, you or your developers have broken that high-level scope item down into individual tasks and functions, such as "validate the username," "verify that they have an active session," "update the mailing address in the CRM," "update phone numbers in the CRM and in the billing application," and "update user's avatar in the CRM, the image asset repository, and the CMS." This is a pretty basic system. But these five tasks should generally take two days per task, assuming that the whole task is going to take ten days.

Since each task estimate is now two days, our check-in for each task is six days before the task is due. This is the essence of the three-times rule. Multiply the effort estimate by three, subtract it from the due date, and use that as your first check-in. That means that if those ten days were scheduled as Monday to Friday, followed by another Monday to Friday, then the first task will be scheduled for Monday and Tuesday, due end-of-day on Tuesday. To check in six days beforehand, means that you will check in on the previous Tuesday morning, first thing. You don't necessarily need to do this for all five individual tasks but starting with the first in a batch of five tasks should give you a good idea of whether it will be on track. If your ten-day task is just one task in a large set of work that's in a year-long project, you'll want to verify that the task is still scheduled as planned about 30 days before it's due (3 x 10 days).

Visually, it looks like this:

	Est. Days	Week 1	Week 2	Week 3	Week 4	Week 5	Week 6	Week 7
		M T W T F	M T W T F	M T W T F	M T W T F	M T W T F	M T W T F	M T W T F
Profile Edit - Milestone	10		▲ 1st check-in		▲ 2nd check-in			Due ▲
Validate Username	2					▲		
Verify Session	2					▲		
Update address	2						▲	
Update phone numbers	2						▲	
Update avatar	2							▲

The ten-day task is due on a Friday, so you work backwards from the due date, and schedule two quick check-ins to confirm that everything is on track. If the individual tasks are significant, you may have check-ins on those as well, but they may not always be necessary. In this example, you'd be checking-in on tasks ten separate times over a two-week period, which might get overwhelming. The two high-level check-ins in weeks two and four might be more than sufficient.

Waterfall: This method works rather well for waterfall development, as most tasks are planned well enough in advance that you know enough details to have a healthy check-in. Even looking at the example above on how to do the check-in, you'll notice that familiar waterfall look: the steps flowing down from the top left to the bottom right. That's the very concept of a waterfall, which is why this method works here.

Agile: This method is a little more challenging for agile, especially if you're working in two-week sprints. In that case, the initial check-in is just a gut check to determine whether anything suggests that the planned sprint, or task within the sprint, is still achievable. But when you are dealing with agile projects, you're probably not dealing with ten-day tasks anyway, so your check-ins on smaller tasks can happen in your daily stand-ups.

The check-in activity doesn't need to be anything more complicated than just checking with the developer, or yourself, to ensure that this routine is still likely to start on time as planned. If the answer is yes, then you're good to go. If it's no, then you have time to figure out why, and to solve the problem. It also means that you have sufficient time to notify project stakeholders if there's a chance that the deliverable's deadline is in jeopardy. Most of the time, you can spend the first half of that advance time just getting clarifications needed to help steer it back on track. The next check-in would be at the two-times mark—in the above example, this would now be on a Thursday morning—and again, you have two more days to make additional adjustments if needed. This is usually more than enough time to make corrections, move other tasks around, or to request changes to the timeline if necessary.

The key is just to make a deliberate point to review at some predetermined set of intervals to ensure that that the project and major tasks are staying on track, and so that you have enough time to adjust before a task is scheduled to start, rather than finding out after a deadline that it isn't complete.

Output

Your output here is relatively simple. At the end of this section, you should have fully functioning, usable code, with most of your major development done and out of the way. From this point forward, you'll be doing more detailed testing and coding any fixes and alterations that are needed to round off the details of your system.

Section 3.3: Reviewing / Testing

Inputs:

- Project Plan

Steps:

- Assess Code Documentation
- Assess Code Function
- Assess Code Efficiency
- Test Code for Unit and Functional Operation
- Perform Integration Tests

Outputs:

- Training Reference Drafts

Like the rest of the development phase, you don't need to hear how to do formalized testing for your development project. As a project manager though, having a full understanding of the testing process and how to report it to project stakeholders is important.

The steps above can be followed in any number of ways. In a formal development environment, there are several automated tools with continuous integration and continuous deployment solutions that will perform many of these tests for you. In a smaller environment, you may not have this luxury, but knowing that this sequence of tests still needs to happen as part of the development process can be helpful. Most importantly, you want to ensure that your developers follow some kind of formalized testing process regularly, as they iterate through the development cycle, because the results of tests are going to be the primary conditions where questions and scope clarifications are necessary. That's the information that you need communicated on a daily basis so that you can follow up with your project owners.

The testing process tends to introduce potential for more scope creep. Remember what I said about developers having a tendency to solve the problem within the problem, and getting off course relative to the objective? This is the area where it happens the most. A developer's tendency is to identify an issue, and then to solve it by adding more code; either by fixing code in an existing function, or by adding new functions to address the specific issue. This isn't inherently a bad thing, since that's the purpose of testing. But there is a tendency for developers to solve problems in complicated ways that might be better solved by challenging the condition that caused it, which means referring back to the original scope requirements to see if anything was missed.

For example, if a test reveals that a SQL query returns millions of records, when the expectation was to receive a maximum of about a dozen, it may call the initial scope request into question. Rather than solving the problem by adding something reckless like `TOP 10` or `LIMIT 10` to a database query, it might be worth bringing it back to the project owner and asking, "are you aware that the data you're seeking has millions of entries in our system?" If that's unexpected, it might reveal that the owner made a bad initial request, forgetting to provide critical criteria.

I had this happen once where a project owner wanted to target individuals with a specific postal code structure. In Canada, where I live, postal codes are structured according to region, and the postal code given to me identified a range for a large metropolitan area of Toronto, Ontario. I neglected to ask whether they had verified that postal code, and the resulting query returned hundreds of thousands of records. This was intended for a mailing. Fortunately, I verified it with them, only to find out they had given me the first three digits of a postal code that started with the letter "M" (the Toronto area), but they actually meant "N", which covers a less populated area west of Toronto, although it's larger geographically. Along with the other criteria in the query, the correct result was only a few hundred records, rather than a few hundred thousand. When your company is planning a mailing to a few hundred people, and you wind up with a dataset of several hundred thousand, and they have a tendency to send their mailings off to a printing company without reviewing the data, it only takes one of those kinds of mistakes before you start verifying every request afterwards.

Here's where you might be thinking, "yeah, we know all this... we deal with this kind of stuff in testing all the time... what does this have to do with project management?"

It matters because in many cases where development is operating in a non-development company, the developer's common tendency is to just plow through issues until they're fixed, without ever rethinking or verifying the problem from the beginning. Sometimes they even implement solutions that aren't necessary, and almost always lengthen the timeline as a result. By raising this in an open communication mentality, and establishing a good communication pattern, this is a perfect opportunity to put responsibility back on the project owner in a way that either solves the issue without unnecessary coding or stress for the developer, or, provides an easy way to notify the project owner that an unexpected result has triggered a scope change and you need an extension on your project.

Now, maybe your project timeline is perfect, and you don't need an extension at all. If that's you, you probably don't need to be reading this book. But if this kind of issue has ever happened to you, you also likely experienced the most common impacts of failing to use that opportunity to request the extension: developers work overtime to fix a problem; developers get stressed trying to solve a problem that was caused by a bad specification; developers solve a problem incorrectly, and inadvertently create another bug that triggers this whole process again.

The point is this: scope creep always happens, and in development circles, it winds up being the developer that has to pull out all the stops to get the problems fixed. Using these kinds of tests to your advantage and putting responsibility back on the owner is a great stress reliever that you can use during your project. Imagine the conversation going a little like this:

You: "Fred, when we were testing our routine for getting that customer data for your report, we found that there are millions of records being returned, and your report is going to take 12 hours to run each time. Knowing that you expected only a handful of results and wanted to run this daily means we need to figure out a solution."

Fred: "Millions of records isn't right. Let's see the data."

You: [hands Fred the data]

Fred: "I had no idea we had all this in the system. I need you to filter out the customers who are over the age of 50, and any that have children, and any who haven't purchased from us in the past three years."

You: "The original requirements didn't specify those filters. It may take a couple extra days to add that criteria in, because that's in different areas of the system. Can we extend the timeline by a couple of days to get this right for you?"

Fred: "No problem. Sorry that I didn't include that initially."

And just like that, you got an extension. I know, I know, real world discussions don't generally happen like that , and Fred may still try to blame you for missing it, but it's a political technique that works more times than it fails, especially when you can point out that the original specification didn't include it, and you only need the extension because Fred brought a change. If they don't give you the extension, they're forced to accept responsibility for any undue pressure that's put on you, or for any other scope items you have to cut. If they do give it to you, they're accepting responsibility for neglecting to provide proper specifications.

Equally as important, this is the time to pad your estimate a little bit. You might estimate that you only need a couple hours to make the change, but Fred doesn't know that. And you can't see the future, so technically you don't know that for sure either. Pad the time, especially if you need it for any reason, and then try to do it in less time. You're better off to request extensions as a result of bad specifications with a little reasonable padding and then deliver early, than you are to request too short of an extension because you short-changed yourself in your estimate.

That's why, in this process, you want to test like your project depends on it. Don't be afraid to use external testers in your organization. External to your development team, I mean. Specifically, people who are more advanced users who know and understand the work requirements and will be thorough in their testing process. Open up your testing environments to them and let them guide you through any missing scope items or change requirements so that you can communicate those to your project owners. The more you practice this, the easier it gets, and the better you'll get at responding quickly and communicating well to the owners. You may still end up creating a scope creep, or unplanned changes, but it also opens you up to requesting extensions or adjustments by leveraging that process with those who control the project.

Output

This is a perfect time to provide some documentation for your users, specifically to cover the areas of training that they may need in order to use your application. I always leave this expectation here because it's easy to forget about documenting for the end user, and it can be a nuisance to try to do that when a project is done and you're otherwise itching to move on to the next project. Things like release notes, change logs, and other similar documents are good to complete at this point.

Chapter 7: Phase 4 - Testing and Deployment

"To those who say that 'if you need testing at the end, you're doing it wrong', would you prefer a Boeing, or are you going Air Icarus?"
- Michael Bolton

While most developers are familiar with requirements associated with staging and releasing a product for users or customers, the details of user acceptance and training at a project level may be overlooked. As a project manager, these sections can have a huge impact on the overall success of your project and should be accounted for in your planning.

The purpose of having a testing and deployment phase is to help you end your project well, because ending well means that your next project will have a higher chance of starting well.

Waterfall: For a waterfall project, the development phase will include a large thrust of significant development, with micro-testing within the development environment. Once you reach the testing phase, you will be doing user- and systems-based testing, where, instead of merely testing individual functions, routines, and small components, this testing phase covers the larger scope of testing that addresses your project's success at meeting business requirements, creating the feature according to user needs and specifications, and ensuring that the project is fulfilling the broader purpose of the project itself.

Agile: For an agile project, the development phase will have been a smaller, more individually focused set of sprints, so the testing phase here will concentrate on the feature integration and micro functionality of implementation. Overall, this will just be a less complicated and less formal version of the larger testing done in a waterfall project.

Section 4.1: Staging

Inputs:

- Source Control Builds
- Project Scope
- Developer Documentation

Steps:

- Establish Alpha Environment and Test to Scope
- Establish Beta Environment and Deploy Alpha
- Establish Staging Environment and Deploy

Outputs:

- Staged Application
- Release Candidates

There's a good chance that if you've built even one application, desktop-based, web-based, or app-based, you have probably created some kind of a test area and have run one or more tests against that application before deploying to a live environment. Despite having a plethora of tools at our disposal for creating testing environments, I still encounter developers who never deploy anywhere except a live environment, and then just hope for the best when testing in production. A proper test environment, even just a rudimentary one, is something you should never overlook. With today's virtualization and containerization options, there's no excuse for failing to create at least one good testing environment.

Keep at least one layer of separation between a testing version of your application and your live version. That means that your application should be able to run in a sandboxed configuration where it may think it's running in a live environment, but everything is self-contained within the container it's running in.

When I used to do a lot of web development, I would often deploy code to the public server in a temporary location, and then use a local script to copy the application into the live location. Since there were regularly challenges and inconsistencies associated with file uploads, especially in less robust environments, this process helped to prevent any issues with copying files into production without taking the application down while doing that.

Officially, you'd never do that, though. Copying files straight into production because a deployment strategy is too cumbersome? Let's move on.

You should be testing locally, in some kind of containerized configuration to make sure that something works before you push it out. All you need to do is to formalize that, call it your alpha environment, and go from there. If you have a team of developers, it can help to push that environment into a more accessible location for your team. By formalizing this, you create a pattern for deployment that lends way to beta and staging environments as well. If you're particularly disciplined, you'll test in alpha, then push your application into beta, and make that system available to more people for testing. Copying from one testing server to another is a lot simpler than uploading manually to your first environment, and if you don't have continuous deployment solutions in place, tied into source control, it provides an extra layer of protection in your deployments as it helps to prevent developers from pushing code straight from their development environment into an accessible production zone.

From a project management perspective, having a testing environment means you also have the perfect opportunity to get sign-offs on your work. Even if you don't think that you need a complicated testing environment for your own testing purposes, by providing a non-production environment for your users to test in, you gain a great advantage in soliciting feedback before you make the decision to move your application live. You give them the opportunity to give open feedback before you've committed to everything, and you open up the lines of communication for signing off and agreeing to your work. In management, this is critical to rolling out your project successfully, but it also creates the opportunity to build trust with your team and to foster an attitude of having an open line of communication with your project owners and users. When it's done well, you, as the project manager, establish yourself as a natural bridge between the product's user base and the project owners, which means you create a process that encourages teams to refer to you as the lead while you continue to deliver solutions for their business requirements.

Take advantage of a multi-environment setup whenever possible to make your testing and sign-off process more thorough. Soliciting feedback from your testing environment allows you to directly associate the scope changes with user requests, and to give you an advantage when you are seeking timeline changes, if you need them. Since it's likely that other kinds of scope creep will have happened at least once during the life of your project, this is a great way to capture those requests and make the choice of either allowing it to be incorporated back into the scope within your original timeline, or to push back to your users and get them to agree to an extension on the project, all of which is triggered by change requests that they have made. Use this to your advantage to extend your timeline and put the responsibility on the project owners to acknowledge when they're the cause of the extension.

At the same time, there's some give-and-take in this, because you may also find that you didn't end up designing to the specifications, and they may be making adjustments, revealed in the testing process, that you should have caught in the first place before attempting to go live. But at least you haven't mucked up production data to find out what you missed. Use those opportunities to extend your scope as needed, but don't forget to maintain enough humility to accept when you might have made a scope error in the first place, and just use the testing as your quality control. Both for the quality of your development work, and for the quality of the project management experience you're delivering.

If you're working on a more agile project, every push to your alpha and beta environments that pass your QA test are an opportunity to push a deliverable into production as well, by deploying to your staging environment, or straight into the live environment, now that you have sign-off.

Output

Staged versions of your system should be fully available to the appropriate users for performing tests in realistic environments. Depending on the type of system you've built, or how complex your project was, this could be a simple deployment, or it may involve several complicated alignments between disparate systems that may also need their own staging environments in place to ensure everything is working as designed. Only make this as detailed as it needs to be in order to ensure your systems are working properly for the end user.

Section 4.2: User Acceptance

Inputs:

- Functioning Applications

Steps:

- Confirm Final User Acceptance of Staging
- Confirm Success of Deliverables

Outputs:

- none

This stage is probably one of the easiest, especially if you provided a lot of testing opportunities with your environments above. The more micro-sign-offs you can get on small features and deliverables, the easier it is to get sign-off on the project as a whole. Contrary to what many, ahem, *older* developers may think, you don't have to deploy a fully completed product when just a single feature will suffice as a release.

The more frequently you can affirm with user acceptance, the easier it is to capture and complete the deliverables with the project owner's sign-off on the product.

This is also the stage where you have a lot of potential for things to go wrong. If you left too many tests until the end, or if you have missed the mark on a lot of the deliverables, getting a final stamp of approval on the product will be harder. When that happens, make a point to get your users or project owners to agree to an additional plan that you can follow after the project is complete, with specific actionable items that will be delivered at a later time. When a project officially doesn't meet all of its goals, it's wise to call out the goals that were met, and just start a new project to clean up the remaining items without all the extra overhead from the first round. If you've communicated well enough along the way though, the odds of needing to pull this card are pretty low.

Section 4.3: Training / Deployment

Inputs:

- Training Reference Drafts

Steps:

- Provide Training Documentation
- Confirm Final Deployment
- Deliver
- After-Action Review
- Capture of Future State
- Closeout

Outputs:

- Training Documentation
- Project Status Report
- Future State Project(s)

The last major section in this phase is to provide the documentation that's needed to close out the project entirely. One of the easiest ways to get agreement on closure—even if the project didn't fully succeed—is to provide some training documentation. I've yet to meet a single high-producing developer who actually enjoys writing documentation, and most completely avoid writing training material like it's illegal.

Granted, you're primarily good at development, so the chances that you're also good at writing training documentation are pretty low. But by taking the steps to at least attempt to provide some kind of manual for your system, you learn two valuable project management skills. Most importantly, it gives you practice at writing and communicating technical things in business terms, which is a skill you need to practice and maintain for every future project because it's the foundation for relating to project owners. Secondly, it gives you the opportunity to view your project from the perspective of your users and their specific needs. Taking the time to write things out in a way they can understand is a great way to help them understand you, while you seek to understand them.

Just don't be careless with it. Take the time to do a spell check, grammar check, and if you have someone in your organization with writing skills (check your marketing team), don't be afraid to ask them to proofread your material for you. While you may not want a full blown editor critiquing your every word, getting a neutral perspective on whether you've communicated your training concepts clearly, and whether you've understood the business requirements will help you on the next project when you try to gather the initial project information.

Planning your next project while you're still working on the current one is a great way to set a precedent for how future projects will go. While the issues and successes are still fresh in your mind, you can prepare new project plans with those conditions accounted for right at the start.

Ask yourself a few questions about this project. What worked? What didn't work at all? What would you like to repeat on the next project? What do you want to avoid entirely to save a lot of heartache? What did you love? What did you hate? Ask your project owners the same things and get their feedback to use for another project. People are lot more forgiving when they're invited to give feedback, if you're genuinely looking for input that you're going to use to make the project better. A few terrible people will take advantage of the opportunity to completely rip you apart, but that's something you need to be willing to open yourself up to. You can't get good feedback if you're unwilling to hear the bad feedback as well.

From that feedback, make an action plan for yourself to resolve everything afterwards. Make a specific to-do list to follow up on each unresolved item and check in with the people affected by them to ensure you took the right steps to resolution.

Most of this process is called an "After Action Review" and you can look up that term online to find various formats for conducting those kinds of meetings and follow-up discussions. Normally, an after-action review is focused on comparing the intended versus actual results. Other variations of this could be a project de-brief, or a project post-mortem.

Output

This is a great time to finish off any last-minute changes to your training documentation from the development phase, and to provide any final reports to your project owners and stakeholders to close out your project.

Before you finalize and close out your project though, make a point to capture all undelivered items in either a new project, or in a maintenance project where you'll keep track of everything that you need to do to continue supporting the product you built. A maintenance project can be one of best ways to keep tabs on the ongoing success of your product. Completing a project doesn't mean delivering it into the hands of your customer and walking away. Now you have the added benefit of continuously improving and updating what you've built, bringing not only added value, but also the opportunity to keep reviewing active projects with your stakeholders and owners to make future projects run more smoothly.

The more solutions you build, the more you will need to maintain, and the more potential you have for being able to grow and expand your team to support the systems and solutions that you're building. If you're a lone-wolf developer in an organization, this can be just the push your company needs to give you the additional staff required to get new jobs done. The more you can document and prove your deliverables, the easier is it is for the company to identify the costs associated with development, and the actual returns they get back from the development time they invested.

Speaking of maintaining and growing your team...

Chapter 8: Phase 5 - Maintenance and Growth

"Most of the effort in the software business goes into the maintenance of code that already exists."
- Wietse Venema

One of the areas that I commonly encounter as an ongoing challenge between software developers and non-software executives or management personnel is failing to recognize that a software project, once completed, needs to be regularly maintained and supported. While most will respond positively to suggesting, "now that I've built it, I need to allocate time to maintain it," few people will fully understand what that means until you spell it out in detail. Many non-developer folks will assume that maintaining software just means installing "updates" once in a while, without fully understanding that unless you are writing code to make those updates, there are no updates to install.

As a starting point, I assume that however much time I spent building the system in the first place, I'll need 25% of that time annually to maintain it. That's my assumed minimum starting point, and then I adjust and tweak it up or down from there, based on what actually happens over the first six to twelve months. For instance, if I spent three months building a solution (about 65 business days) then I assume I will need to spend about sixteen business days a year maintaining it. And that's just for general maintenance. If that's a bit of a hard number to swallow, or if your leadership team doesn't understand that, consider a few of these conditions, as this can help them to see where that assumption comes from:

- If you've developed a web-based system, then over the course of one year, the following changes have probably taken place: two of the most popular browsers (at the time of writing this, that's Google's Chrome, and Mozilla's Firefox) will have released about eight to ten different versions. Any one of those versions could enable, or disable, some kind of functionality that affects your application. At a bare minimum, you need to retest your application in each version. That's at least 20 cycles of testing every year, and that's not accounting for other browsers, or any other change conditions like security threats, or changes to any frameworks or libraries that you included in your system.
- If you've developed a native desktop or mobile application, the most popular operating systems (at the time of writing this, that's iOS and Android for mobile, and macOS and Windows for desktop) will have likely released one or two major updates to how the operating system works. That's at least two or three additional major tests and potential rounds of changes.
- If your application is SQL-based or uses a programming language that has frequent updates like security releases (common for scripting languages, like PHP or JavaScript), you've likely had anywhere from two to six database or language updates in that time frame.

By the time you add up all of those update cycles and apply your testing phase to your software, it's not hard to see how you can easily spend about three weeks a year maintaining a system that took you three months to build. None of that even accounts for any bugs that legitimately crop up with your users at all, as well.

Section 5.1: Support

What's the best way to support my software from a management perspective?

Steps:

- Recurring training
- Bug fixes

When developing software in a company that doesn't develop and maintain software as a core discipline, supporting software is rarely considered or factored in to your daily work. When you're estimating on developing new solutions, it's easy to forget that you still need to keep that system functioning amid operating system upgrades, desktop upgrades, new technologies, and security threats, and making it all work with all of the other systems you've put in place.

There are two disciplines you need to be good at in order to provide great support for your software: training, and bug fixes.

Spend Time Retraining Your Users

You will definitely be maintaining and supporting your system for a lot longer than you would initially expect. As you do, make sure to update your release notes, and take a little bit of time to retrain the users on any of the changes you've deployed. This has two main advantages. First, it gives you a little more face time with the people you're writing software for. I know, you'd probably rather have the face time with your computer. But taking these steps to retrain a user tells them that you care about their use of the system, you want to help them succeed (after all, why are you developing systems for them in first place if you don't care?), and you want to help them get better by showing them the areas where the system has improved.

Second, you gain an opportunity to get direct feedback which you can then use to refine your own skills in turning ideas into code and then into systems. If you are taking the time to help retrain a user on the changes you've made, they'll usually take the time to share a little more about what they'd like to see as well. Don't disregard their ideas. Some of them may not be possible, but everyone's ideas have value in making sure the product works well for them. Take their idea, triage it so that you can assess its priority, and then treat it just like you would every other bug or request that comes in. Schedule it during the BAU times. When you can return to someone a week, or a month later after they somewhat casually mentioned an idea to you, and you can say, "hey, remember that request you made a while back about the layout of this form? I changed it to what you suggested, and just rolled that out this morning." They'll love you for it. They'll buy you cake, and burritos, and coffees. Well, maybe not, but they'll be pretty happy. You learned something, they learned something, and you've accomplished the whole purpose of project management: managing expectations well.

Get Good at Bug Fixing

You've worked hard on your software and released a mostly bug-free product. But inevitably new bugs are going to crop up. The longer your software remains in operation the less likely you are to have self-induced bugs catch you off-guard. Meaning, bugs that are not a result of external factors like an OS upgrade. That means that the majority of your bugs are going to happen shortly after you launch your product. This is helpful because it's also the time when you're the most familiar with the code, because you literally just finished writing it. Tracking down bugs is easier at this stage, so it's important, when building your system in the first place, to account for bug-fixing time even after the product has gone live. Don't consider the project to be complete until after you've dealt with the largest bulk of bugs. This will give you the opportunity to fix most of the major issues while you still have full dedication to the project and aren't being pulled away on different issues.

In order to get good at bug fixing though, you need to follow five important steps:

1. **Learn to triage.** When a bug comes in, take a maximum of five minutes to assess the importance, categorize your bug (identify which area of the system it's in), estimate the time it will take to solve (refer back to estimating in chapter four), identify its urgency or priority, and then move it to whatever task list system you're using to track your issues. If you can confirm the bug's validity in that same five minutes, go for it. Now put it out of your mind.
2. **Schedule time each week to deal with bugs.** Remember how we accounted for 25% business-as-usual in our estimates above? That's where these fit in. If you regularly have a staff meeting on Mondays, for instance, it might help to reserve a block of time before or after the meeting to deal with bugs. Just make sure you set aside enough time to deal with some of the larger bugs. Any bugs that are estimated to take more than four hours to solve may need to be broken up into smaller tasks to ensure you don't wind up making them a massive project.
3. **Regularly test and deploy.** Don't accumulate a bunch of bugs and try to do major releases. Just fix what you can, during scheduled times, and get it deployed. Even if it's not completely perfect, the habit of regularly fixing and deploying will speed up your processing time.

4. **Regularly compare your estimates and actuals.** Every bug should have a time estimate before you begin. Compare your estimate to your actuals and keep track of that each week in a spreadsheet. Just a column of estimates, and a column of actuals will suffice. You don't need even need to track per bug; just keep a total of all that week's estimates, and a total of that week's actuals. If your project management software can do this for you, then use that, but a spreadsheet is usually sufficient. From that, you can run a basic formula to calculate the percentage difference between your estimate and your actual. Just divide your estimate by your actual. Values greater than one mean you underestimated. Values below one mean you overestimated. After several weeks or months of this, you can calculate the average of your estimates and actuals, to get an accuracy factor. Then, as you estimate, you can make adjustments according to your accuracy factor. For example, if you regularly overestimate by 10%, then you know to multiply your estimate by 0.9 next time. Eventually, this will normalize itself. You'll start naturally estimating at the 90% rate, meaning that you'll eventually be *underestimating*. This will cause you to start padding your estimate by a small percentage, and over time, your estimates will get close enough to the real thing that your backlog of tasks will have reasonably accurate estimates on how long a fix will take. Factoring that in to your scheduled bug-fix time will help to ensure you can make the best use of that time.
5. **Never give up on your schedule.** The habit of setting aside time regularly keeps you in the practice of dealing with bugs, solving problems that are unexpected, and pushing out updates. This means that your documentation and release notes (you do those, right?) stay up to date. It also sets a pattern of expectations for your organization as to how regularly you will keep improving their systems.

Eventually, as the overall number of bugs diminishes for each product or system you build, the amount of time you need to spend dealing with those bugs each week also diminishes. This gives you some advantages when it comes to planning your time and your projects. Any new products you started to build while you were also dealing with trailing bugs from a previous product, can now have more time devoted to them. As the bugs on older systems go away, the newer systems will start to have their increase of bugs, and you can balance the time between multiple systems.

Further, if you aren't regularly cranking out many new products or systems, you can continue to reserve the bug-fixing time to improve your software, or to implement new features, enhancements, and other changes for which you otherwise can't set aside time. This gives you a little more control as you can manage your own work a little more flexibly, but it also sets a good standard organizationally because it manages the expectations regarding your overall availability and how much time you can dedicate to new project initiatives. Few people complain that a new initiative is taking longer than they want when you are regularly maintaining and supporting your old systems and continuing to meet their expectations for most new ones. After all, if timeline is an issue on a new initiative, your choices are to cut scope or increase budget, not to cut into your BAU time.

Getting good at fixing bugs means you're also going to get better at adding new features and providing enhancements. And if you've worked in to a good routine of regularly communicating with users and retraining them whenever you make a system change, or fix a bug, you're well on your way to providing a solid maintenance plan long-term.

Section 5.2: Maintenance

How can I maintain my software long-term especially while building new solutions?

Steps:

- System integration and reviews
- Third party product comparison and assessment

Maintaining software well also means keeping good notes and documentation. We all know that documentation is one of the first areas of development that suffers when building new systems under a rushed timeline. Hopefully, with all of the aforementioned techniques, you're already mitigating the rushed timeline issue. But it takes a lot more self-discipline to also manage your documentation skills, especially if you're the only developer.

But what's the point in documenting things if no one else will read them? I'll remember what I built when I need to!

Wrong. Stop kidding yourself. You'll never remember what you built. How many times have you looked back on your code that's six months old and said, "what was I thinking? Why on earth did I build it this way?" Furthermore, you never know how long you're going to remain at the company. If you leave, and the next person to come in has to deal with a pile of rapidly written, undocumented code, you can pretty much kiss your reference from the company goodbye. Noted software engineering expert John F. Woods described the need for writing clean code: "Always code as if the guy who ends up maintaining your code will be a violent psychopath who knows where you live." Without documentation, your code may as well be written in Latin. Because you're a developer, and it's your job to leave your unique signature all over everything you do, the next developer won't have any trouble tracking you down if they need to. The last thing you want is for them to be Woods' psychopath.

To get good at documenting, just keep practicing. You don't get good at it by writing it perfectly on your first try, just like you don't get good at piano by sitting down for the first time and trying to play *Flight of the Bumblebee*. Make a point to document everything. If you don't have a great documentation tool, pull out your text editor. There's nothing easier to maintain for a developer than a text file, because every coding utility can work with it. Even better if you can use something like markdown, which is still just straight text, but many markdown editors can also render good exported documents without doing any fancy formatting. Keep your documentation right inside your code repositories. You can add a `/docs/` folder, or just put a README file in each folder. Whatever works for you, but keep the files handy at all times, and keep them up to date.

The best way to ensure you take the time to do that is to treat documentation like bugs: explicitly set aside time regularly to focus entirely on documentation. Ideally, you should spend a little bit of time each day. Perhaps even just half an hour. Or maybe it's how you spend Friday afternoons. Use a pomodoro timer (search for one), and train yourself to document for 25 minutes, then take a five-minute break. Repeat three more times, and you've spent two hours documenting from 3pm to 5pm on a Friday afternoon when you are otherwise—let's face reality here—surfing the web looking at cat videos and fail videos just waiting for 5pm to roll around while also complaining that you never have time to get all your work done. Make better use of that time.

Reviewing Your System

When you're doing the bug-related work, or other minor improvements, take the time to verify that your product is still working as designed in the environment that it's in. Perhaps you built an application for a specific version of an operating system, and that system has since been upgraded. If you regularly review the systems, and keep your documentation up to date, you are less likely to get caught off guard by a major issue that grinds your system to a halt.

Knowing how much time to set aside to review your system personally is important. As I mentioned, I recommend starting with 25% of development time over a year. Try to break the intervals up into reasonable chunks. If your project required 48 days of work, you need 12 days a year to maintain it. You can either allocate a single day per month, or about two hours per week, whichever method works best for your schedule. Set that schedule and stick to it. You don't have to use 25%, just pick a number as a starting point, work it into your BAU percentage (which you account for when calculating your project's entire timeline anyway), and then stay on the schedule. You can always revise it if it's not enough, or too much. Keep in mind that if you start with 25% of your development time, that's the actual development phase you're comparing to, not the architecture or testing phases.

Compare to Off-The-Shelf Products

It never hurts to regularly compare your system to off-the-shelf products. I've personally experienced plenty of times where I've developed a solution for an organization, because nothing off-the-shelf was available, only to find out a few years later that a viable alternative was now available as either a standalone product, or as a web-based application. Regularly reviewing other software solutions provides you with several benefits.

You have the opportunity to improve your own system by comparing it to the features available in a commercial product and revising your own feature backlog. Being able to reinvest back into your product by developing features similar to a readily available system gives you leverage with your organization for being able to invest more time and resources into maintaining your system. This is a huge advantage if you're at that tipping point where you need more staff, but you're having a hard time convincing the hiring authorities that extra staff is justified. Further, it provides you with reasonable data for any proposals you want to put forth for requesting time to be allocated to expanding the feature set or performance of your system.

You can compare the cost of continuing to maintain your system with the cost of purchasing or leasing a commercial product instead. This can work to your favor. You may be able to identify that the cost of switching from your custom-built system to a commercial system will save the company money over time. In some cases, perhaps even immediately, depending on the commercial offering and your current cost of maintaining. By making this kind of switch, you gain the benefit of continuing to deliver a reliable solution for your company, while also freeing up the previously allocated maintenance time you've been spending on it. Alternatively, it may affirm for you that the cost of continuing to maintain and service your existing system is still cheaper than the commercial product, which further justifies the ongoing maintenance costs as well as any potential future investments you want to make in the system.

Either way, all of this information carries weight when reporting on the ongoing success of a product with your management or executive teams. Keeping your solutions in a constant state of review gives you the opportunity to leverage that data in a way that is beneficial both to the organization's best interests, and for your interests as a project and product manager to ensure that you are continuing to keep the organization's needs as a top priority.

It never hurts to keep it as a humility and accountability check as well, and for most of us, that's a necessity to keep doing our jobs with integrity.

Section 5.3: Growth

Steps:

- Iterative enhancements
- Iterative new features
- Backlogging
- Future version planning
- Cycled releases
- Communication strategy

Let's assume you've completed the primary development on your application or system, and you've worked through the majority of your bug backlog, as well as most additional minor feature requests. You're now at a point where you've effectively declared your project "complete." Although it might feel great to put your feet up and switch to another project, and put this one behind you, it's a great idea to account for growth options and opportunities for this project. There's one reason why I would highly recommend that you factor this in as part of your overall project's plan right from the start: even though you may be done development, and have no new features to implement, the system that powers your solution is likely to change underneath you, and if you don't account for that, you'll be stuck dealing with a change at the worst possible time. Nothing saps your energy more than getting stuck dealing with an old software application because some part of its foundation crumbled away on you.

If you've built a web application, the browsers are going to change. If you've built a standalone desktop application, the operating system is going to change. If you've built a device-independent system that runs through a virtual machine, the language, platform, frameworks, or virtual machine requirements are going to change. Maybe not within a year, but in five years, there's a good chance you're going to be facing a hefty upgrade process. If your solutions are regularly built on the same platforms with no plan to migrate off of them in the future, you may find several years down the road that you're stuck replacing an entire mass of systems all at once, without any capacity to accomplish it. All it takes is a single software vendor making a large infrastructure change, or a platform being bought out by a company that only wanted to acquire the engineering talent, and suddenly your implementation is out of date without support, and you have a bunch of company executives asking you every day why you aren't done yet.

While this doesn't happen frequently, if you have any plan for longevity at your organization, it's something you should at least account for, even if all you do is to prepare a basic plan for when that kind of condition occurs. From the following steps, you don't always need to apply every one of these for every project. These are all contextual based on whether any of these steps are suitable for the project you've just completed.

Planning for Iterative Enhancements

Enhancements are changes to your software that improve existing functionality. You are building on solutions you already have but improving the experience for the user. This might be a purely visual upgrade to make the UI more modern than it was when you built it. It might include changing the layout of a form to make it more intuitive for the user. It might include adding support for features that are now considered a standard for the operating platform you built it on. One great example is when you build the software with a standard UI, and suddenly the OS you built it for changes its UI to support a new window layout, or to introduce "dark mode," and unless you adapt, your system immediately looks like yesterday's news. Whatever the reason for making an enhancement, the point is to keep your mind active on the current software implementation and to regularly check on its compatibility with generally accepted standards. The last thing you want your software to be called is "old school."

Planning for Iterative New Features

In contrast to enhancements which improve existing functionality, new features are completely new functions built into the system that didn't exist previously. One of the best ways to improve an existing system is to merge its functionality with another custom-built system, so that users can run a single solution in one place, rather than using multiple tools. While this is more common in standalone systems that had single-purpose functions to them, it's also common for web-based solutions that couldn't be built out into full blown applications but can now be merged into a unified tool.

One common issue I've encountered with custom software solutions in a non-software company is the concept of what I call "utility drift." This is where a one-off solution needs to be built, and you have to provide some kind of interface for the user to work with. An example of this might be something like a utility to process an incoming payment log from your payment provider, and to convert that log into another format to be ready for import into your accounting software. At some point, you have to build some kind of interface that provides this conversion for your end user, and a web-based upload-and-download process might be suitable. Then, months later, you need to build another utility to handle the import of online order data into your CRM, because your website orders can't be connected directly to your company's archaic CRM solution. Now you've built two completely different interfaces for handling essentially the same process: translating data from one format to another, via file uploads and downloads. Ideally, these should be merged into a single system, manifested as a consistent UI that allows for easy maintenance and modifications if the connecting systems ever change their data formats.

This kind of scenario is a perfect example of needing iterative new features. Not only are you increasingly more likely to require additional interfaces that will convert and migrate data from one source into another—especially if your company is heavily dependent on working with data from remote sources or cloud applications—but you will also want a single, unified interface with security restrictions to ensure that everyone who is authorized to use the utility has access to it. Migrating individual systems into a single, maintainable system is a great long-term plan for adding new functionality to your solutions.

Planning for Backlogging

As you continue to maintain your system and account for enhancements and new features, you should also regularly review your backlog system. There are always ongoing enhancements to task-management and bug-tracking tools such that you can invest in a basic issue tracking system and know that it will be maintained for a long time. You don't need anything overly complicated. If you were in a software development company, it makes sense to invest heavily in an advanced bug and feature tracking system. In a non-software company, with a small or single-person development team, this is probably overkill. The data produced from analyzing bug and feature progress over time doesn't contribute much to your project management needs, nor does it provide enough data for the organization as a whole, when most managers and executive leaders aren't overly interested in fine-tuning the productivity of the development team. They just care about whether you're getting their requests done in a reasonable time, and within budget.

Be willing to switch backlogging systems as needed, so that you can easily triage and handle your incoming requests well. Any tool that will let you capture a task, assess it, and set it aside for later processing based on priority, will be sufficient. Don't be afraid to keep upgrading or switching your system, even if it means exporting and transferring all your logs a few times over.

Planning for Future Versions

For the past 15 years or so, "agile" has been the popular word applying to most development projects, and for whatever reason, the word "waterfall" in reference to a more traditional project has been treated like a dirty word. The biggest difference between the core principles of waterfall and agile is that waterfall usually involves a long, heavily invested project with a less flexible scope, while agile is done in shorter sprints with the ability to change the scope more easily. Which method you are applying simply affects the technique you use on planning for future versions of your software. Just because you implemented your first version as a waterfall project, doesn't mean you can't use agile to maintain it. Similarly, you may have released your first version—or perhaps, your first several versions—in an agile manner, but that doesn't mean you're prohibited from implementing a waterfall solution later on.

In a waterfall project, you might spend months building a solution, and then release version 1.0 of your system. If you're planning for future versions, you're likely to release a 1.5, or a 2.0 version at some point, and potential ongoing plans from there.

In an agile project, you're more likely to do a waterfall delivery upfront, to create your 1.0 version, but from that point forward, you are doing regular, agile deliveries, incrementing from 1.0 to 1.1, 1.2, 1.3, and so forth.

What's most important though, regardless of the methodology, is that you're making a point to track and document your various releases. This is important for project communication, because you can identify additional large projects, or micro-projects, where you can attach an explicit software version to your deliverables. When your users see that the version is now available or released, they have some definitive release notes, documentation, training material, and support information available to them, which not only improves your overall communication with them, but also gives you the opportunity to maintain that backbone of development—documentation—that you would otherwise ignore.

From a project manager's viewpoint, planning for future versions means that you can take all of those notes that you captured during the development process, add the scope items that you set aside but didn't complete, and add the brainstorming items that weren't applicable during the first round of planning, so that you can put them into a future release project, if appropriate. This allows you to take all the leftover junk that usually gets forgotten about and recycle it back into a new project. A few months or years after your software has been released, you may find that many of the ideas that were previously disregarded now have a lot more value and can be planned out for a future release.

Planning for Cycled Releases

If your project has more of an agile focus, this is a great opportunity to take some time to schedule several cycles, or sprints, of new releases. Even if you've completed the entire backlog on your project, there will undoubtedly be new items that will crop up that you simply don't want to focus on, or where the organization has a few ideas but the ideas aren't mature enough yet to justify spending development time on. By plotting them into cycles for release in the future, you can at least do some of the early research to help move the ideas along, so that when you are ready to put time into it, you've got everything organized. You never know when you'll reach a point where you have no pressing work to do for a few weeks and pulling out an already-planned release to work on might be just the time filler you need between projects.

Planning for Communication Strategy

Depending on your organizational structure, you may also wish to set aside time to conduct a more business-level review of the software and make decisions about what additional value the system brings to the organization as a whole. Regularly communicating about the software's impact, how it's continuing to improve internal workflows, or reduce staff time helps to remind the organization as a whole about the benefit of continuing to invest in your systems. In particular, identifying how your software requires, say, three hours of user interaction per week, where the previous manual method required 40 hours a week, can be a great reminder that the system is regularly saving the company 37 hours of manual labor, reducing errors, and contributing to an overall more efficient workflow.

Knowing this helps to remind the company that ongoing investment into development is beneficial to everyone.

*****

Overall, the point of all of the continued growth planning is to put yourself in a position, as a developer and as a project manager, to protect the long-term integrity of the system when conditions change, and to protect yourself and your team from after-release scope creep items that wind up becoming massive volumes of unplanned work that consume too much of your time. By being proactive in your management of tasks and planning out future iterations, even when the company isn't asking for it, you keep yourself ahead of the requests and remain in control of the process while still respecting the company's expectations for future builds.

This process is a great way to deliver expectations and keep your stress levels low as you continue to manage your ongoing list of projects.

Chapter 9: Conclusion and Summary

As a developer, most software projects are going to be second nature to you, at least when it comes to building and deploying a software solution for your organization, since it's something you can practically do in your sleep. But the nuances and details of software project management can still be challenging, especially if administrative requirements are not your natural strength.

The purpose of this book has been to help you apply knowledge that you probably already had as a developer, and to add on the requirements needed to also succeed as a project manager. Like any skill, project management needs to be practiced regularly. You can't just pick up a project here and there, apply a few basic principles, and expect to master it quickly, in much the same way that you can't learn a programming language, write a small utility, then switch to doing carpentry for a few years and expect to be able to jump back into coding as though you never left. Not using the skill means you're going to lose a little, or a lot of it, over time.

To be good at project management, just like being a good developer, you need to exercise the skill regularly, and apply the principles in more than just a small handful of projects. I would recommend applying these project management skills to even small projects that only require a few days or a week's worth of work. Even though the process may seem large and complicated, the habit of regularly stepping through the phases, sections, and tasks as a to-do list can help to lock in the mentality on what is required to see a project through to completion. It doesn't need to be complicated, but following a prescribed list can help.

In order to do this well, you need to keep working through the guidelines in this book repeatedly and make them a constant habit. My hope, in wrapping up everything you've learned through this book, is that you'll have not only enough of an understanding of the process to make it second nature to you, but also that you'll be able to apply these principles and practices quickly, efficiently, and without feeling any administrative burden. The goal is for this to become such a natural workflow for you that you gravitate automatically to this process and see results no matter how small or how massive your software projects are. Mastering these skills with even the tiniest of solutions ultimately means you'll perfect it on the most complicated ones, and you'll be able to work through the entire system without feeling any of the pressure or stress that you would otherwise feel.

So how does this whole process work for tiny projects?

As overwhelming as the entire process may seem, the reality is that each phase can be as short or as long as you need it to be, although I usually stick with a rough idea of an evenly distributed timeline as a guideline. Phases one and five will be however long they need to be to get the job done. Phase one may take only a few hours, maybe a few days. But there are plenty of opportunities before the end of phase two to revise and re-scope the project, with the owner's buy-in, making it easier to account for all of the scope changes that will naturally come up. For a project that will take a month or several months to accomplish, it's good to devote at least a day or two to phase one. But for a project that will only take a few weeks or a few days, you only need a couple of hours to complete that phase.

By that time, you'll have a reasonable estimate on the remainder of the project's length. Since phase five takes place after the project is completed, and may exist in perpetuity, you only need to account for the timing on phases two through four. As a guideline, I always assume that each phase will take one-third of the project's overall length. Within each phase, you have three sections. Each of those takes one-third of the phase. And within each section, you have several tasks. Each task should usually take twice as much time as the task below it. It looks a little like this:

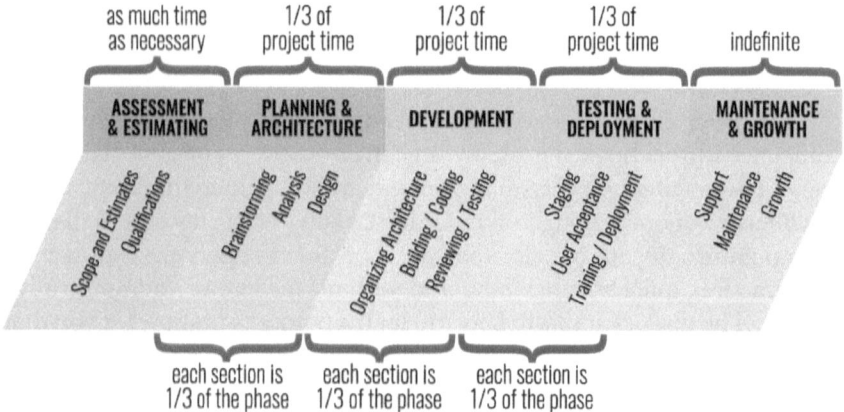

For a waterfall project, this breakdown is fairly straightforward. Each section is one-ninth of the overall project length, so if your project is nine months long, you should spend one-month brainstorming, one month doing analysis, and so forth.

One question I hear on this structure is, "wait a minute... if this is a nine-month project, that means I'm only spending one month doing building and coding?" Although it appears that way in theory, and this can be off-putting to a developer who "just wants to write code," the actual coding process begins in the Design section, and continues to the Reviewing/Testing section, as well substantial coding and bug-fixing work in the entire Testing and Deployment phase. So that really means you would be spending between four and seven months actually writing code.

To calculate the time you should spend on individual tasks, the estimating is a little trickier, but becomes simple once you get the hang of it. You can also use the following guide as an example:

PLANNING & ARCHITECTURE - 33% overall		
Brainstorming	**Analysis**	**Design**
33% of phase, 11% overall	33% of phase, 11% overall	33% of phase, 11% overall

Brainstorming		Analysis		Design	
Initial Concepts	57%	Develop Business Scope and Charter	51%	Establish Business Use Cases	50%
Organization and Structure	29%	Proof of Concept	25%	Define Development Parameters	25%
Gather Requirements	14%	Validate Requirements	13%	Define Test and Scenarios	13%
		Develop Project Scope	6%	Develop Conceptual Models	6%
		Establish Budget and Timeline Constraints	3%	Define Business Processes	3%
		Define Project Plan	2%	Develop Interface Wireframes	2%
				Validate Design Concepts	1%

DEVELOPMENT - 33% overall		
Organizing Architecture 33% of phase, 11% overall	**Building / Coding** 33% of phase, 11% overall	**Reviewing / Testing** 33% of phase, 11% overall
Define and Document Core Architecture — 53%	Develop Logic Flows and Functional Sequences — 57%	Assess Code Documentation — 52%
Establish File and Code Structures — 27%	Develop Functional Implementation — 29%	Assess Code Function — 26%
Define Development Templates and Patterns — 13%	Build Unit and Functional Tests for Scenarios — 14%	Assess Code Efficiency — 13%
Design Class and Object Structures — 7%		Test Code for Unit and Functional Operation — 6%
		Perform Integration Tests — 3%

TESTING & DEPLOYMENT - 33% overall		
Staging 33% of phase, 11% overall	**User Acceptance** 33% of phase, 11% overall	**Training / Deployment** 33% of phase, 11% overall
Establish Alpha Environment and Test to Scope — 57%	Confirm Final User Acceptance of Staging — 67%	Provide Training Documentation — 51%
Establish Beta Environment and Deploy Alpha — 29%	Confirm Success of Deliverables — 33%	Confirm Final Deployment — 25%
Establish Staging Environment and Deploy — 14%		Deliver — 13%
		After-Action Review — 6%
		Capture of Future State — 3%
		Closeout — 2%

The percentage beside each step in a section represents the amount of time you should spend on that step relative to the section as a whole. Using the nine-month project as an example, the Development phase should take about three months. The Reviewing/Testing section should take one-third of that, which is one month. Assuming a month is about 22 working days (176 hours), then the step of assessing code documentation would take 52% of that time, which is about 91.5 hours, or about 11.5 days. The step of performing integration tests should take 3% of 22 days, which is just over five hours. Again, these are just guidelines, but it gives you a rough idea of what is a reasonable amount of time to spend on each step.

For the mathematically-inclined, here are the calculations to work through, to determine how long each task should take:

1. Count the number of tasks in the list. For instance, in the Analysis section, there are six tasks.
2. The base unit for the bottom task will be equal to 2^n-1 (where n is the number of items in the list) and then divide that number into the estimated time for the section. The bottom task in the Analysis section is "Define Project Plan".
3. Now, each additional task above the bottom task will take twice as long as the task below it. Multiply the base unit by 2^m where m is the number of steps away from the bottom step.

Sound confusing? It's not too bad once you try it a couple of times. Let's go through this with the example used above, but let's use a shorter timeframe of nine weeks instead of nine months.

- Assume that the project estimate is that your entire project should take about nine weeks to complete.
- Phases two through four should each take 1/3 of the time, so phase two will take three weeks.
- Sections one through three in phase two (Planning and Architecture) should each take 1/3 of that time, so section two ("Analysis") will take one week. In order to make it easy to calculate fractions of a week, let's refer to this in hours: 40 hours.
- In the Analysis section, the number of tasks is six, with the bottom one being "Define Project Plan."
- Since n=6, we can calculate that base unit: `40h ÷ (2⁶-1) = 40 ÷ (64-1) = 40 ÷ 63 = 0.63`. Based on this, the project plan should

take approximately 0.63 hours to accomplish. This is just a little shy of 40 minutes.

- Based on this, we then know the following for the other five tasks:
- The task above, "Establish Budget and Timeline Constraints", is one position away from the bottom task. Thus, m=1, so the time required to accomplish this task is `0.63h x 2`^{m}` = 0.63 x 2`^{1}` = 0.63 x 2 = 1.26h`. The second last task will take 1.26 hours, or about 75 minutes. Of course, you can just double the final task to get this answer, but it does require working your way up through the list to calculate each one.
- Repeating upwards, the third last task is two positions away from the final task, so m=2, and the total time is `0.63h x 2`^{2}` = 2.52h`
- The remaining tasks, working up, will require 5.04, 10.08, and 20.16 hours respectively. Thus, the first task in the section will take the most time: just over 20 hours. When you add those up, you get the full 40 hours of the entire section: `20.16 + 10.08 + 5.04 + 2.52 + 1.26 + 0.63 = 39.69 hours`. It's a little over 15 minutes shy of the full 40 hours, but that's mostly due to rounding.

If you want to be a super geeky developer about this, you can always write an Excel spreadsheet to do all those calculations automatically, so that you only need to plug in your total estimate, and let the formulas calculate the approximate amount of time you should spend on each task. Overall, most of these calculations aren't really needed, since you can refer to the percentages calculated above in the diagrams.

Remember though, that this is just a guideline. It should tell you how long you should aim to spend on a task as a starting point. It might take longer, or it might take a lot less time. But if you're working through your project and realize that you've spent 35 hours this week on a task, but the estimate said you should have spent about 20 hours, you are probably jeopardizing your project, and wasting time unnecessarily. Use the guideline to help rein in your thinking and to keep you focused.

How does this all relate to a tiny project? In the example, we used a nine-week project as the estimate, mostly because it's easy to do the math, dividing nine by three, and then divide three by three. But what if your project is only going to take a week? Should you still do all the tasks? Well in some cases, you can skip tasks entirely if they don't apply. A small project, for instance, may not need a project charter at all. Or maybe the charter is just a single sentence, or a single paragraph. Getting in the habit of applying all of the steps regardless of the project will help to keep the process engrained in your mind, which makes it easier to apply it on bigger projects when you need to. It also establishes a pattern of consistency for your project owners.

Using a smaller project as an example though, let's take that one-week project, and express it in terms of hours. If you're spending 40 hours on a project, you should be spending about 13.3 hours on planning, 13.3 on development, and 13.3 in testing. Your brainstorming section should take about 1/3 of the 13.3 hours, so about 4.43 hours brainstorming is reasonable. For each of the steps in that section though, you'll spend about 2.5 hours on Initial Concepts, 75 minutes on Organization and Structure, and about 40 minutes on Gathering Requirements. This adds up to about 4.4 hours, which is a good way to spend a Monday morning, as you complete the entire first section of your project.

When you break everything down into small chunks and limit the time you can spend on each section (while giving yourself a little bit of flexibility on the task time), you can easily press through a small project while following this process from beginning to end.

So, what should I do differently for exceptionally large projects, or for projects with lots of people on my team?

If you can adapt this for small projects, you can adapt it for massive ones as well. The same rules apply as it does for a tiny project. Spend as much as time in phase one as you need to, and once you reach phase five, you can determine how long your maintenance and growth plan needs to stretch out based on how long you intend to support the product. For particularly large solutions, you may wish to aim for at least a 10-year support cycle.

For phases two through four, you want to make sure that everyone involved is working according to the same set of standards and guidelines. Teach this process to all your developers and designers, as well as everyone else who has a major stake in the project. They don't all need to be experts in knowing the process, but they do need to know enough to recognize that there is a process, and that as the project manager, you're responsible for making sure it's happening. Communicate well with them, and don't leave it up to every individual to figure it out on their own. Guide them through it, lead them, and encourage them as they go. Encouraging your team doesn't mean simply saying, "I encourage you to do X...". That's just a fancy way of saying "do what I tell you," and it's rarely received well. Instead, if you're genuinely encouraging someone, you're identifying their strengths, reminding them that they are good at what they do, and making sure they have the opportunity to use their strengths to make the project succeed. When they accomplish their own work with excellence, point it out. Remind them that their success is contributing to the team's success. When they get their work done well, and done on time, others can pick up the next chunk and get their work done well and on time too.

For extra-large projects, always break it down into smaller sized chunks. This is back to the "how do you eat an elephant" philosophy. The larger the task, the more overwhelming it tends to feel. The more you can break it down into smaller pieces, the easier it is for people to latch onto and work through it on schedule. It's a lot easier to get a week-long task done in a week when you break it into ten smaller, four-hour chunks. It also makes it easier to identify when you're going off course, or when the timeline is in jeopardy, because a four-hour task that winds up taking six hours is more likely to mean that every other four-hour task needs 50% added to the timing.

By compartmentalizing everything into manageable tasks, it becomes a little more natural to check in regularly and to ensure everyone is on target. It's also less awkward to bring up issues when there are failures or shortcomings, since you only have minor issues to address. This can help you to remain calm when there are failures and problems, because you don't have massive deliverables jeopardized that create worry for the team and cause everyone's blood pressure to go up. Instead, you'll experience small, manageable issues that you can deal with calmly and graciously, one at a time. The smaller the task, the smaller the impact of failure, and the less likely you are to have a complete meltdown when something goes wrong.

When something does go wrong though, own the issue. It's your job to help put out the fires, so if there's a specific person to blame, deal with them personally, but accept the overall blame on behalf of the team. Conversely, when there's a major win or a huge success, point back to the team to acknowledge their work.

What if my company doesn't care about all these details? Why spend the time doing all of this extra work if no one else cares?

There will be companies that pressure you to deliver quickly, and you'll feel coerced into skipping the formal process in favor of just getting the job done. More often than not though, that approach doesn't work. Not only does it force you to just be a code monkey that is constantly cranking out code without long-term vision in mind, it also sets a pattern for how large projects should be handled. By delivering well on small projects, you can provide a pattern for your own process that will help encourage others in your organization to see the process as valuable, since they'll see great communication and processes that deliver results. If you can take the time to prove the process in a few test projects, you'll be in a much better position to negotiate your timing so that you can apply the process formally in other settings and with much larger projects.

Imagine, for a moment, that you are asked to build a shed, and as soon as you arrive on the job site, the home owner tells you to just grab a saw, a hammer, some nails, and to start nailing boards together to make a shed. There are no instructions, no guidelines, and no architectural plans or expectations; instead, just a demanding owner that is yelling, "Build it! Build it! Build it!" while you frantically scramble to piece together something resembling a shed, but which will collapse in a couple of weeks as soon as there's a strong wind or a rainfall. Obviously, this is an absurd example, but sometimes, on the receiving end of a pressured project, it can feel like that's exactly what's happening.

The lie we have bought into as developers though, is that the product or project owner is literally standing there shouting "build it!" while looking over our shoulders, when in reality, they're not doing it at all. The feeling of pressure may be fabricated, and we manifest it in our minds as the absurd example, when what's really being requested is, "please get this done as soon as you're able." We inflate the pressure to assume it means "now" instead of using the opportunity to help define for them what "when I'm able" actually means. So now it's up to you to decide how you're going to accomplish it. When it feels to the owner that you aren't getting things done, it's probably because you legitimately felt pressured, assumed that you were being unreasonably constrained, and then acted on the assumption by madly coding something, anything, just to shut them up. Taking a step back and planning the project out properly ensures that you include the owner in the process and gives them some insight into what you're going to do for them. It further gives you the opportunity to buy yourself the time you need, and to establish a healthy conversation between you and your team, and between you and the project owner. Communication is the key to ensuring the project succeeds and that you're granted the time you need.

How do I recover when I fail?

No matter how hard you work at this process, there will be some projects that simply can't be accomplished in the time frame, or that go sideways after you've started. While you may try to account for all of the possible exit paths, and how to fail gracefully, you can't always account for failures that are a result of a complete failure of staff to accomplish the work, or for situations where extraneous circumstances arise and your organization simply chooses to halt or cancel the project, with no opportunity to close it down properly. These kinds of situations are rare, but they do happen, and you still want to fail gracefully when they do. Here are a few tips for how to fail with some dignity.

Most importantly, stay humble. Don't take the opportunity to point out everyone else's faults—even when it really is their fault—as a way to deflect blame from yourself. After all, they might have legitimate reasons for pointing back at you and if you aren't prepared to take at least some of the blame, don't start shifting it to others. The more you can encourage and support others when things go wrong, the better you can come out of this.

However, I'm also not an advocate of allowing yourself to be trampled on, professionally, when there is clearly a single person or a group of people to blame for a project's failure. Or maybe no person is to blame, but there's an underlying system or process that is completely wrong, and it caused team members to implement a failed solution. Perhaps you butted heads with other developers because they refused to follow processes. Maybe your own supervisor is clueless to your work and refuses to listen when you raise concerns. Maybe the project owner has completely unreasonable expectations and refuses to acknowledge mistakes even when it's clearly documented as to where he or she went wrong. Whatever the situation, if you really do need to point blame at someone else because your job is on the line if you don't, then do it with some degree of respect and dignity. Don't let it get emotional, and don't use any information other than hard facts. If you bring statements like "I feel like Joe was not focused on the work" or "I think Mary was unable to understand the magnitude of work and pressured us too much," then you are bringing too many subjective values into the conversation.

Stick with well-documented (you did that, right?) facts like, "I raised this issue with Mary on February 10th and her response was to ignore it unless the issue comes up again. I raised it when it happened again on February 23rd, and her decision was to ignore the issue because it was low risk. It occurred a third time on March 2nd, and we had a full system failure, so I raised it with Mary, and she reprimanded me for failing to identify it as a serious enough issue earlier." Try to avoid casting an opinion on the person's competence, but rather state what went wrong and don't be afraid to mention names as long as you have it well documented. As soon as your documentation comes into question, so does your integrity and your credibility, so make sure you have the facts before you need to point blame.

When the mistakes are legitimately yours, don't be afraid to admit those proactively as well. The more you can identify your own shortcomings and areas for growth voluntarily, the less likely you are to be accused of it by someone else, because you've already self-identified the issue. Take ownership of any failures that you can, even when minor, because it will make it easier to accept ownership for the big things when needed. Use a phrase like, "I failed to provide enough support to ensure my team could do the work, so I'm planning to focus on more frequent support discussions on the next project." With every project, if you identify learning areas for yourself—even if they are just things you learned, and not necessarily failures—you create an atmosphere of open discussion where others will recognize that you are open to receive healthy and positive criticism, rather than someone who is closed-off to learning and growth. It's equally important to identify how you will address those issues in a future project, by identifying what changes you'll make to ensure you don't repeat the problem. Sometimes, just the small steps of identifying areas where you could improve, publicly to the team, creates a less tense environment when deeper discussions are needed.

To address some of the biggest failure issues, instead of making point-blank accusations, try asking questions that provoke and demand a humbling response, rather than outright blaming. For instance, if one team member was not pulling their weight and someone else had to constantly pick up the slack, try asking the slacker a question like, "when the workload was heavy, and your team was relying on you, what method did you use to ensure you were carrying your share of the workload?" This is a non-personal question and encourages the person to identify their own systems and processes, which deflects the accusation away from them as a person and directs it onto their work habits and performance without getting emotional. Sometimes, asking a question like that opens up the discussion to reveal things about the person that might shed light on their lack of contribution. I've asked questions like that in the past, while on the inside, my mind is screaming, "what kind of a fool are you that you don't realize how much you slacked off?!"

In one case in particular that I experienced many years ago, where I could feel my own blood pressure rising with a team member who was not pulling their weight on a project, I ended up finding out that this person was going through some major family issues at home. They knew full well that they weren't contributing as much as they could have, but they were scared to raise it during the project because they feared losing their job, which would have worsened the home situation. I felt like the world's worst project manager when I learned this, because I had been aggressively pressuring this person to complete tasks on time, when all it would have taken was a pair of open ears to realize that they were producing slowly because their family life was a mess. Even without knowing those details, a question like the one above would have helped to identify that this person didn't even have a system for dealing with the workload, because they were too mentally exhausted each day to be as productive as they needed to be. But instead of asking, I was pressuring to complete the work, and as a result, they didn't feel empowered to raise the issue they were going through. It only came up in a somewhat casual discussion where another team member had the courage to ask, "what's not working for you that I can help with" and the developer came right out and said, "my life."

Taking time to understand the other person's world can help to address some of the biggest points of failure in a project: when people are too stressed to work effectively. And it's equally important for you to check in on yourself to ensure that you are working to your fullest, and not causing your own burnout. Make a point to open yourself up to the same kinds of questions that you need to ask your team members, so that you can keep your own performance in check as you go.

At the end of everything, make sure you ask a few bold and inviting questions to solicit feedback on your own work. If you're an expert developer, but you're reading this book because you're not an expert project manager, don't get your expertise mixed up. You are a great developer, but you are not, yet, a great project manager. So, when you solicit feedback, aim to improve the area where you need the most growth and learning, and invite feedback there, while sticking to your strength in development. You have the right to command and direct the development discipline, the technologies, the languages, platforms, systems, frameworks, and architectures. But in project management, I assume, this is where you want even more feedback so that you can eventually gain that expertise. Try asking some of the following questions:

- What could I have done to recognize these issues sooner?
- Were there conditions or identifiers that you feel I missed that could have given me insight ahead of time?
- What resources could I have provided to my team to keep them on track?
- What scope items or requirements did I miss that caused us to miss this issue?
- What did I misunderstand about the scope that made this seem smaller than it was?

It's never easy to admit fault, or even to open the door to accepting any portion of blame, but remember that everyone else is in the same position. When a project fails, it's the team as a whole that suffers, but you want to keep yourself in a position whereby you maintain a level head, a neutral frame of mind, and a humble attitude. These traits will serve you much better on future projects than having an attitude of anger, accusation, or blame-casting on others. Look for the opportunities to improve and take the criticism—and the praise—when it comes.

Final Thoughts

As overwhelming as software project management can feel, my hope is that this system helps to give you a process that makes it easy to get a better handle on how to deliver projects on time, on budget, on scope, and with as little stress and pressure as possible. In providing this system, I hope that it encourages those of you who are fantastic developers, but who face struggles within your company trying to deliver on everything that's expected of you while maintaining your own sanity and health through the process.

As with all skills, this is something that you only get good at by practicing it, and by incorporating it in to your daily routine. Keep at it, apply it to all of your development work, and take the time to keep your mind active and productive so that you can deliver with confidence.

I wish you all the best on your development endeavors, and may all your projects finish well.

Appendix - The Entire Project Structure

As a visual guide, this entire process is available online at http://pm.stevepye.me. The lifecycle is available in a board format, a sequence layout, and a task layout, so that you can view the same list of tasks in whatever format makes the most sense to you.

For quick reference, the project structure is available here.

Project Outline and Timeline Breakdown

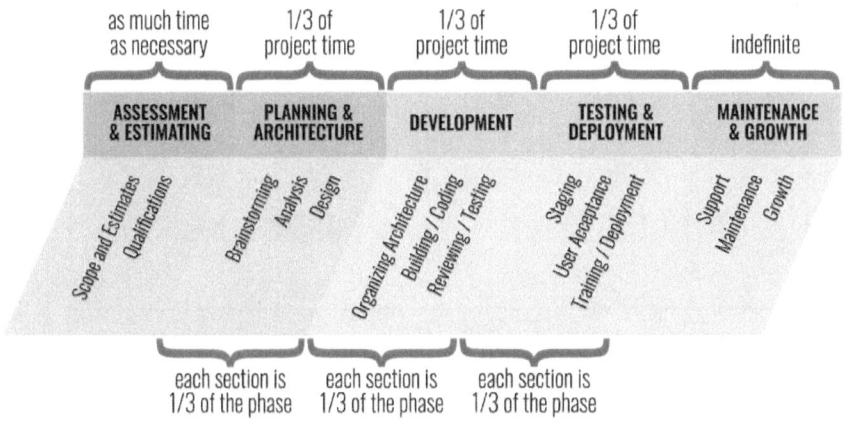

Assessment & Estimating

ASSESSMENT & ESTIMATING	
Scope and Estimates	**Qualifications**
Identify Scope	Assess Importance
Estimate Baseline Effort	Identify SMEs
Quantify Tasks	Identify Assumptions
Normalize Tasks	Identify Urgency
Prioritize Tasks	Establish Deadlines
	Assign Workflow

Planning & Architecture

PLANNING & ARCHITECTURE - 33% overall		
Brainstorming 33% of phase, 11% overall	**Analysis** 33% of phase, 11% overall	**Design** 33% of phase, 11% overall

Brainstorming		Analysis		Design	
Initial Concepts	57%	Develop Business Scope and Charter	51%	Establish Business Use Cases	50%
Organization and Structure	29%	Proof of Concept	25%	Define Development Parameters	25%
Gather Requirements	14%	Validate Requirements	13%	Define Test and Scenarios	13%
		Develop Project Scope	6%	Develop Conceptual Models	6%
		Establish Budget and Timeline Constraints	3%	Define Business Processes	3%
		Define Project Plan	2%	Develop Interface Wireframes	2%
				Validate Design Concepts	1%

Development

DEVELOPMENT - 33% overall		
Organizing Architecture 33% of phase, 11% overall	**Building / Coding** 33% of phase, 11% overall	**Reviewing / Testing** 33% of phase, 11% overall
Define and Document Core Architecture — 53%	Develop Logic Flows and Functional Sequences — 57%	Assess Code Documentation — 52%
Establish File and Code Structures — 27%	Develop Functional Implementation — 29%	Assess Code Function — 26%
Define Development Templates and Patterns — 13%	Build Unit and Functional Tests for Scenarios — 14%	Assess Code Efficiency — 13%
Design Class and Object Structures — 7%		Test Code for Unit and Functional Operation — 6%
		Perform Integration Tests — 3%

Testing & Deployment

TESTING & DEPLOYMENT - 33% overall		
Staging	**User Acceptance**	**Training / Deployment**
33% of phase, 11% overall	33% of phase, 11% overall	33% of phase, 11% overall

Staging		User Acceptance		Training / Deployment	
Establish Alpha Environment and Test to Scope	57%	Confirm Final User Acceptance of Staging	67%	Provide Training Documentation	51%
Establish Beta Environment and Deploy Alpha	29%	Confirm Success of Deliverables	33%	Confirm Final Deployment	25%
Establish Staging Environment and Deploy	14%			Deliver	13%
				After-Action Review	6%
				Capture of Future State	3%
				Closeout	2%

Maintenance & Growth

MAINTENANCE & GROWTH		
Support	**Maintenance**	**Growth**
Recurring Training	System and Integration Reviews	Iterative Enhancements
Bug Fixes	Third Party Product Comparison & Assessment	Iterative New Features
		Backlogging
		Future Version Planning
		Cycled Releases
		Communication Strategy
		Training and Marketing

About the Author

Steve Pye is a father of four and has worked for over two decades in software development, business management, and project management capacities in a variety of industries including automotive, manufacturing, software development, insurance, and non-profits. As an experienced developer and project manager, he has led projects ranging from small developments to multi-million dollar ventures.

His passion lies in helping businesses succeed through effective process management and utilizing project management and systems development practices to build solutions that provide the maximum in long-term sustainability.

When he's not spending time with his family, Steve enjoys reading, hiking, board games, and exploring the world of technology. Steve lives in Ontario, Canada.